Charles Middleburgh

The Zebra's Hoof

**'Thoughts for the Week' during the Pandemic for
The Dublin Jewish Progressive Congregation
2020 – 2022**

Hakodesh Press

Imprint

Any brand names and product names mentioned in this book are subject to trademark, brand or patent protection and are trademarks or registered trademarks of their respective holders. The use of brand names, product names, common names, trade names, product descriptions etc. even without a particular marking in this work is in no way to be construed to mean that such names may be regarded as unrestricted in respect of trademark and brand protection legislation and could thus be used by anyone.

Cover image: Provided by the author

Publisher:
Hakodesh Press
is a trademark of
Dodo Books Indian Ocean Ltd. and OmniScriptum S.R.L Publishing group
Str. Armeneasca 28/1, office 1, Chisinau-2012, Republic of Moldova, Europe
Printed at: see last page
ISBN: 978-3-639-79455-7

For the members of the Dublin Jewish Progressive Congregation, past and present, whom it has been my honour to serve for over 20 years

and

For my beloved wife Gilly, z"l, who made my life complete for 40 years

Table of Contents

INTRODUCTION

The Covid-19 Pandemic, still far from over, has dramatically changed the world. In microcosm, as with other faith communities, Jewish communal life has been profoundly affected.

For many months synagogues were shut with as many activities as could be replicated online moving to Zoom. While the technology took some getting used to, and has its detractors, I am not one of them. Zoom offered my congregation in Dublin a means, not of total liberation from the circumstances in which they found themselves, but of connecting with friends and fellow congregants which they would not otherwise have had.

I went online with DJPC (the Dublin Jewish Progressive Congregation) from the Shabbat after lockdown in March 2020, and over the many months that followed weekly and festival services helped create a sense of online community of which we would otherwise have been deprived.

Very early on I needed to decide what to do about sermons: it seemed obvious that the standard 10-12 minute sermon in the synagogue would be an ordeal online. I decided to restrict myself to between 650 and 750 words maximum, which equated to 5-6 minutes, a reasonable period of time for my congregants to sit through in their little Zoom boxes. It also offered me a challenge to see whether I could create a much shorter piece of writing that contained all the necessary elements that make a sermon satisfying and thought-provoking. I decided that it was necessary to give these pieces a different name to distinguish them from a classic sermon, and Thought for the Week (TFTW) seemed as good a choice as any.

This volume contains the TFTW's – and two poems - given between March 2020 and May 2022, the last delivered in person in Dublin.

Charles Middleburgh
Leo Baeck College, London

Freedom in Lockdown

There's never been a *Pesach* like it, and hopefully there won't be another one!

How extraordinary! Here we are celebrating *zeman cheyruteynu*, the season of our freedom, and we are doing so in lockdown, our *sedarim* a pale shadow of their normal, rambunctious selves. For me this is like a return to childhood, once again I am the youngest person present and have to recite the four questions! (Technically speaking my dogs are younger but they're still wrestling with Aleph Bet.)

The words we recite around the table will take on new meanings this year and when we get to the Ten Plagues I suspect many families will add an eleventh, perhaps with a *toi,toi,toi* to ward off the evil virus. Transitioning from slavery to freedom will be harder than ever to engage with when we have had our freedom severely restricted, albeit with a very positive intention.

This enforced home time does give us an opportunity to reflect on the key themes of this season in a modern light. How we enslave ourselves to work, how we graft for 'stuff', new cars, new laptops, new kitchens, exotic holidays, new phones for all the family; how all too often we self-validate on the basis of our material possessions rather than on our qualities as a human being. And we do have qualities, even though they are more obvious in some people than others.

The juxtaposition of *Pesach* with a real plague in 2020 should encourage, or force us to engage in some real introspection, the sort that we usually associate with the Day of Awe. This should be a wake-up call of a most serious kind, with a message we ignore at our peril. For far too long, and increasing exponentially in every generation, we have become selfish and self-obsessed – what's in it for me? is the question we regularly ask ourselves – we don't instinctively think in an altruistic manner, considering the needs of others, rather do we seek to bend everything and everyone to our own advantage.

So when the circumstances change, and the opportunities for feeding our self obsessions diminish or disappear, we become frustrated and resentful, as exemplified by the idiots who thronged public spaces over last weekend in complete rejection of the instructions of their government not just to self-isolate but to socially distance. You can hear the thought process in some of their heads as it travels between one brain cell and its solitary companion: it's really nice outside, I need some exercise, I need to see my mates, so what if this blows up efforts to control Covid-19, as long as I stay illness free what else matters?!!!

As we know from the Exodus story, the Israelites did not embrace their gift of freedom with unqualified enthusiasm, in fact they complained almost from the start. So what if they were free but food, or water, or creature comforts were in short supply! They had them all in Egypt! Slavery? Well, it wasn't easy but at least we knew where we were!!

There are two monumental misunderstandings about Passover: one about its purpose and the other about why it took so long for the Israelites to enter the Promised Land. The first is an error easily made, after all this is the 'Season of our Freedom', but in spite of the extent to which the Almighty went to liberate the Israelites from Egyptian servitude, their enslavement was not the over-arching reason for their liberation. God redeemed Israel from slavery in Egypt to be enslaved to God through the covenant at Sinai. When Torah entered the world, said the Sages, freedom entered it [Bereishit Rabbah, Vayera 53.7]. God did not want Israel to be free for the sake of it, but specifically to receive and wear the *ol shel Torah*, the yoke of the Torah, a servitude gifted at Sinai to every generation of Jews to come for all time. This means that the greatest act of liberation is the one that happens inside each of us, when we find a way of living our lives that works.

The other misunderstanding is why it took the Israelites 40 years of wandering before they could cross the Jordan into the promised land. We remember the story of the spies sent from the 12 tribes to see what the Promised Land was like. They came back with two messages, and that from the majority was bad – there was no way they could possibly defeat the people already occupying the land, and it wasn't that nice a place either!

So all that generation, with the exception of Joshua and Caleb who gave the minority report, had to die out before the conquest could occur: no one not born into freedom could do what was necessary.

I believe however that this is just a blind; the real reason is much deeper, much more challenging, and much more likely.

You might assume that having a common enemy – the Egyptians – would have meant that the Israelites were united. But having a common enemy can cut both ways, and it is more common for everyone to try and do a deal with their persecutors, if at all possible. In this endeavour one's fellow sufferers are the competition at best, and the enemy at worst. Liberation doesn't switch that outlook off, because these coping mechanisms are deep-rooted.

What needed to die out was indeed a slave mentality, just not the one we think usually of; the Israelites needed to learn to co-operate, to make sacrifices for the greater good if that was required, to have a personal stake in their neighbour's success not just in their own.

Set against the backdrop of COVID-19, hidden away in our own little bunkers, it is all too easy to slip into a 'me me me' mindset. Yet this is something which we must resist if we are to unlock the greater truths in the Passover story.

Like the Israelites we are on a journey, like them we are fearful of what may lie ahead: but unlike the slave generation we care for each other, we yearn for each other to be well and stay well. This Pesach, more than any other in my lifetime, we need to retain our altruism, our fellow feeling, so that in the future, when the pandemic has passed, we are united in heart and mind and can carry on together.

Pesach

8th April 2020

Echoes

There is a radio station in the UK called Classic FM. It's been around for 25 years and I remember listening to it on the very first day. It has done an extraordinary job in bringing classical music to a wider audience, and it has also encouraged more staid classical stations, notably BBC Radio 3, to popularize music more than it ever has.

Every Easter Classic FM have a four day extravaganza called the Hall of Fame 300, when they ask their listeners to nominate their three favourite pieces of classical music, and the number of votes cast dictates the place in this classical chart. It is the largest exercise of its kind in the entire world and has listeners across the globe, including, I am sure, here.

For the last few years Gilly and I have paid close attention to the Hall of Fame, up to and including the piece that clinched the number 1 slot. This year being the 250th anniversary of the birth of my *primus inter pares*, Ludwig van Beethoven, whose music I prize above all others, I did hope that he would reign as supreme in the chart as he reigns in my musical heart, but alas no. The number one piece of music, and it has been number one for 10 of the 25 years that the Hall of Fame has been running, was The Lark Ascending.

Why this extraordinary dominance?

My childhood was spent on the South Downs of East Sussex, a short walk from my home in Hove where I was born and spent the first 21 years of my life. The down land is a perfect place for Skylarks to nest, and at the right time of the year no walk with the dog took place without the serenade of the skylark as it took off from the ground and soared into the air on wings of song. It is a glorious and complex melody, indeed the lark's song has been analysed by science and it has been shown to sing no fewer than 230 notes per second!! No other European bird except the nightingale has more complex song.

The composer Ralph Vaughan Williams was similarly captivated by the skylark's song, creating a 15 minute gem called The Lark Ascending that, as I remarked, is this year's number one piece on the Classic FM Hall of Fame.

It is a beautiful work and an intensely evocative one. When I listen to it I am transported back to childhood walks on the Downs with my parents, indeed so evocative is the piece that for a number of years after my father died I couldn't bear to listen to it.

Why, though has it proved so popular with Classic FM listeners? I don't KNOW the answer but I suspect that it is because the piece, written in the year the First World War began, 1914, evoked a simpler life, a purer life. After all the years that have passed I suspect that the yearning for a simple life has not been vanquished by hi-tech sophistication and the internet. When we hear The Lark Ascending we are reminded that a simpler life can be full of real pleasures.

One of the few bonuses of this crazy time in our lives is that the absence of traffic on the ground and in the air, has enabled us to hear bird song, the best natural sound there is. Who would have thought that such a miracle existed when it was drowned out by human noise?

If you search for healing, and you have the wherewithal to do it, go outside in the early morning and listen to the birds. You may be surprised by the echoes their song evokes in your heart, and the simple pleasure it brings to your stressed and troubled mind.

15th April 2020

Ketev Meriri or, The Pangolin's Revenge

Since ancient times we humans have been terrified by
the killers we cannot see.
Justinian's Plague, The Black Death, The Plague of London.
Strange to note how often blame was laid at *our* door.
Strange how the notion of long-held revenge created the absurdity
of the Jew as fomenter of death.

And now Corona. *Plus ça change.* Once again we are damned
as guilty by fascists and other gullible fools.
Yet this is not about us, though there are men and women
whom history will judge culpable.

They are not history's whipping boy, they are the consumers
of animals endangered by their greed and heartlessness.
It took just one threatened pangolin, in the wrong place
at the wrong time, eating some food contaminated by a bat.

The person who bought the pangolin, had it killed and brought it home,
imbibed the virus that has become a blight upon the earth.
The beautiful pangolin could not have known the outcome of its mischance meal,
And even if it had I don't believe
it would have been driven by joyful revenge for the persecution of its race.

We should swallow this bitter pill and change our ways.
We should learn the meaning of the fear that invades our hearts.
We should be afraid of the swirling pestilence
that has slashed its way across the globe.
We should be afraid that our lives will never be the same.

The greatest irony?

Many thought that global warming would change

the world.

Many thought the seas would claim us, the floods, the quakes.

No one foresaw that nemesis would come from one small scaly creature.

The Bible talks of *Ketev Meriri*, a whirling pestilence,

a bitter death, destined to humble humanity.

Who could have known

 that it would be our generation and our time

that would feel God's lash,

for our arrogance,

our cruelty,

our fecklessness?

19th April 2020

Memento Mori

For too long we have driven
the winged chariot of purblind progress,
cut a swathe through earth
and cleaved the heavens,
none hindering our advance.

In our arrogance and our triumph
we have failed to hear, 'til now,
the age-old viral voice susurrating
in our ear:

Memento mori, human,
remember you are mortal.

19th April 2020

Soft sounds in the void

How strange are these times through which we are living. How much time we have for leisure. How much time for introspection. How much time to reflect on the way we have lived our lives. How much time we have to think about and plan for the future. How hard it is to have any clear idea of what the future will be like.

Yet how uncomfortable it feels to have everything going on around us without being able to engage with it, change it, do anything at all! How painful to learn of businesses in crisis, institutions closing down, the pillars of our normal lives creaking swaying and sometimes crashing to the ground.

It is very hard in the new world that has been forced upon us to be positive hopeful, convinced that this nightmare will end one day. History, however, shows us that this will happen, epidemics do die down, vaccines will be found, immunity will be built up. The cost in human misery and human lives, already high, may be unbearable but we will soldier on because that is part of the makeup of every human being, we will rise to the challenges of a re-ordered world.

When the prophet Elijah fled from the wrath of King Ahab and Queen Jezebel he journeyed to Mt Sinai and hid in a cave on the mountain. He desperately needed a sign from God, some reassurance that everything would somehow sort itself out, after all what could be more reassuring than God's assurance? There came a mighty wind, but God was not in the wind. There was an earthquake that shook the mountain, but God was not in the earthquake. There came fire, but God was not in the fire. Then there came *kol demama daka,* a soft, murmuring sound, and Elijah knew that this was the voice of God.

Silence is now a regular quality of our 'new' lives. Let us use it well. Let us listen in the silence, to the sounds not of aircraft, or massive trucks, but to nature, to birds, to insects; and maybe we too will hear *kol demama daka,* the soft, murmuring sound that is the voice of God.

20th April 202

Stopping the Rot

Decay is often a problem: a window sill surround the wood of which has gone rotten lets in the rain. A door frame that is rotten can make the door easy to break down. Tooth or gum rottenness can be almost exquisitely painful and send the sufferer for some even more painful, and expensive, dental treatment, often involving extractions and root canal work.

I'm sure you get the picture! The problem with discovering rottenness is that it is, always, a problem. Involving time, expense, and a great deal of stress.

The section of *Tazria-Metzora* that I read this morning contains the only reference in the Tanakh to decay in a building, describing what we today would call dry rot or rising damp. In ancient times it was a priest who took on the role of surveyor and came and checked the building out, returning a week later to see how things had progressed. If he deemed it worthwhile all the rotten plaster was removed to be replaced with fresh plaster, but if the damp or dry rot returned then only drastic measures would suffice. The building would be demolished and the rubble taken outside the camp and dumped in what was known as an 'unclean place'. The rottenness that had destroyed the building was dangerous, it was contagious and it need to be placed away from human cross contamination.

In the new reality which we now inhabit, we have a whole range of new words and phrases, as well as some very old ones, that have entered our daily vocabulary. We talk of social distancing, of self-isolation and lockdown; we refer to ICUs, ventilators, swab tests as if we were seasoned medics; we talk of the virus, Covid-19, coronavirus and the plague.

In this terrifying new world humanity responds to threats and adversity in similarly new and old ways. Some panic, become paranoid and anxious; others embody a cool accepting attitude which then engages with ways and means of making things right, if that should be possible.

The latter harness everything at their disposal to come up with solutions, the best and biggest minds are focused on finding a solution; the feckless act true to type, ignoring advice to practice social distancing, acting as if they cared nothing for anyone, except perhaps themselves, and possibly making the overall situation worse for everyone.

Being composed of people, governments show all these traits: and as the speed and severity of Covid-19 has made it impossible to contain the virus, have been playing catch up with varying degrees of success. At some point in the future, I imagine almost all democratic countries will have inquiries, and their findings are likely to do terminal damage to some political careers – a tiny price, of course, when measured against the tens of thousands of dead.

The worst will be, as has today begun to emerge in the UK, when a government knew that its people were vulnerable to a new pandemic, and that its hospitals, doctors and nurses were shamefully ill equipped to deal with it. When it is known that a clear warning was issued but ignored, many societies and many countries will demand a price be paid and that should be concerning.

As a result of Coronavirus it has been demonstrated to all of us that life can be turned on its head in a matter of hours. If, as is now being suggested, we may have to live with Covid 19 not for a few weeks, or months, but potentially years, new structures, new ways of living will become essential. The stuff of our carefree, pre-Covid lives – shopping centres, restaurants, pubs and cafes, may no longer be able to function as they have in the past, and many of them will go to the wall. Foreign holidays could become a thing of the past, air travel will be irrevocably changed, and we will have no choice but to accept it.

In biblical times, the contagious quality of rottenness was understood, and needed to be eradicated and removed from human life; today we need to remove the rot represented by Covid 19, but it may be a very long time before it can be contained.

25th April 2020

Don't worry - be happy!

Like many rabbis, and most people, I am concerned with Coronavirus, the damage it is doing to our lives and livelihoods, and the threat it poses to our future on so many levels.

In such a climate no rabbi would wish to be thought detached from everyone else's concerns by ignoring them and focusing on something else. Yet after last Friday and Saturday's services I said to Gilly, I think I need to talk about some other things too. So that is what I am going to do, even though, like everything else, it does have a direct Covid connection.

At a time when cinemas are closed, as are theatres and concert halls, we have to find ways of not just entertaining ourselves but of rising above our situation. For some that will be binge-watching series or movies on Netflix or Amazon Prime; for others it will be by reading as many escapist works of fiction as you can handle; for yet others it will be by listening to music. And for some of us it will be all of those and more.

I decided that I was going to make myself a playlist or two that I could listen to when I wanted uplift. I decided to call it Happy Songs and set about thinking what I wanted on it. Some things came immediately to mind: from my all too solute youth, it was a question of deciding which songs by the Beatles, the Stones, Joan Baez, Bob Dylan and others to choose.

From other times of my life it was Bob Marley, The Who, Three Dog Night and Bachmann Turner Overdrive. Then I had to have some songs that were not just evocative but made me smile as well, even laugh: so Monty Python was added, as was a lot of Flanders and Swann (and deciding what to leave out of their back catalogue was a nightmare!) and Kenneth Williams. That was the easy part, but as I started thinking I was inundated with other names: Tom Lehrer and the Goons had to be in there, so did Elvis, Elton John, David Bowie, Bruce Springsteen, Tom Jones, Simon and Garfunkel, Tina Turner, Aretha Franklin, Ella Fitzgerald, Louis Armstrong, Paul Simon, Don Maclean.

I checked and found that I had about 7 hours of music. Fantastic!

Ah yes, but then I was horrified by those I had left out.

So ABBA came in, as did Sky, John Williams, Noel Coward, Sinatra, Gershwin, Topol, Ute Lemper and the Treorchy Male Voice Choir, and the next time I checked there was over 12 hours of music, at which I stopped.

What's the point? The point is that we are all living our lives in a completely unnatural way against a backdrop of threat and anxiety about the future. We have to work hard not to be overwhelmed by the uncertainty of it all and we need things that lift our spirits.

Music has that rare ability to transcend time and circumstance, to take us out of ourselves, to remind us of things long forgotten, to get our feet tapping, to make us smile. And boy do we need things that make us smile these days!

So I encourage you to compile your own list of Happy Music. Give it some thought, you'll be amazed at what surfaces straight away; and what emerges once you're in the groove may astonish you further. And use it, and let your mood be changed; enjoy discovering yourself grinning. It will cheer you up no end.

As the late, great, Bobby McFerrin sang: don't worry, be happy… a sentiment to which I will give a heartfelt Amen!

2nd May 2020

Gotcha!

Almost anyone using the internet is familiar with encountering something called CAPTCHA when first trying to connect with a new website. Some know, though others may not, that CAPTCHA has only been around since 1997. And the acronym? Well, it isn't a cute way of spelling capture, the letters do actually stand for something, though when I spell them out to you in a moment you'll probably wish I hadn't. CAPTCHA stands for Completely Automated Public Turing test to tell Computers and Humans Apart. You see what I mean?!

Nevertheless, CAPTCHA does fulfil an important function, enabling websites, in many cases, to protect themselves against bots by generating tests that human beings can pass but computers, so far, cannot. You usually see a photo of a US street scene in which you are asked to tick the boxes in the overlaying grid that have traffic lights, or buses, or zebra crossings. Get it right and you're in, fail, even by missing one small thing and you have to start all over again. And simple though it is it does require real concentration if you don't want to endlessly repeat the exercise as you get more and more frustrated and more and more distracted.

At some point during this past week I registered with a new website, I have no clue now what it was, but I had a pleasant surprise. Up popped the CAPTCHA logo with the little box for ticking but above it were words that I hadn't seen before. They read Give Proof of Your Humanity! That brought an all-too-rare-these-days big smile to my face. Addressing my Mac I told it, 'my dear, I hardly know where to begin... and if you think I can testify to my humanity in a box that would struggle to contain a gnat you are much mistaken'.

Perhaps Give Proof that You are Human would have similarly amused, but not nearly as much. Clearly, the clever clogs who came up with a brilliant new phrase thought they had found an elegant, fresh way of framing a long standing internet question.

If under Give Proof of Your Humanity, there had been a large empty box with an infinite number of allowed letters, I suspect that the answer would have taken a long time to write, combining personal opinions, religious teachings and a fair amount of modern and ancient philosophy. Alas, none of this was possible because in spite of asking a massive question all there was room for was a tick. So I ticked and was in.

Give Proof of Your Humanity is a very big ask at any time, especially in the era of COVID-19. Those brave people in the emergency services, and in hospitals, prove their humanity often by giving of their utmost, up to and including their lives. Captain Sir Tom Moore gave eloquent proof of his humanity by embarking on a venture that has raised at least 32.8 million pounds. Others give proof of their humanity by delivering food to neighbours, or skyping or zooming or facetiming those in isolation. Others do it by the eccentrically new British ritual of emerging on their door steps at 8PM on a Thursday and banging saucepans, cheering the workers in the NHS.

There are plenty of people, in Ireland and in the UK, who give daily proof of their humanity in the most wonderful ways. But it is not enough for us to bask in the humanity of others, we need to give proof of our **own**. We need to think not just of what we have done since the shutdown in our families, we need to think what we have or should have done in this community, for fellow congregants, some of them friends for decades. We need to think of what more we could do, for our neighbours, for our friends, and for strangers. And then we need to act.

So ask yourselves this Shabbat, what proof have I given of my humanity in the past week and, depending on your honest answer, decide this week to do something positive, helpful and human for others.

8th May 2020

Butterfly wings

There has been a spike, it appears, in sales of books that are about plagues, particularly *The Plague* by Albert Camus and Gabriel Garcia Marquez' *Love in the Time of Cholera*. We are, of course, not suffering from a plague of cholera, but that's where it all started. And the original culprits? Unsurprisingly, perhaps, the British.

On the Bay of Bengal there is a vast area of tidal swamps called the Sundarbans, renowned, *inter alia*, for its man-eating Bengal tigers. It was taken over by soldiers of the East India Company in the 1760s, when they captured Bengal, and a decision was taken to make far better use of it. By the 1810s no less than eight hundred square miles of forests had been razed and during the rest of the nineteenth century people moved into 90% of the Sundarbans. So what, you may be thinking. So quite a lot, I must reply.

Once the eco-habitat of the Sundarbans was effectively destroyed tiny crustaceans called copepods – just a millimeter long – came into contact with people in ways they never had before. A major problem because they carried the bacterium *vibrio cholerae* and once crustacean-human collision had occurred the bacterium jumped onto the human in what scientists call zoonosis.

What made cholera into the global pandemic it became was not local infection, it was the jump to European, especially British, people, who carried the bacterium with them when they travelled back to the Old Country, and everywhere else for that matter.

There was a local pandemic, however, in 1817, after a very heavy rainfall when copepods and their bacterial passengers washed into people's homes, farms and wells, with an R (reproduction) value of between 2 and 6. And within a matter of months 00,000 square miles of Bengal was infected with cholera.

As we all know, cholera is a devastating disease, almost always fatal without treatment, and mounts a rapid assault on the human body causing a range of horrible outcomes before death occurs. As sea travel became more and more widespread so did *vibrio cholerae*, often travelling not just in humans but on copepods unwittingly picked up in infested waters as ships' ballast.

In our own time, globalization and the breadth and ease of air travel, makes the creation of a pandemic a matter of hours rather than weeks or months.

I suspect some of you remember the epitomisation of Chaos Theory in the much misunderstood proposal of the meteorologist Professor Edward Lorenz, expressed in the early 1970s. Speaking to the American Association for the Advancement of Science, he said that a butterfly flapping its wings in Brazil could cause a tornado in Texas. Over the years the theorem has been shrunk to a frequently used phrase '*the butterfly effect*', but in its application today it fails to express what Lorenz was actually proposing, which was that complex dynamic systems can exhibit unpredictable behaviours so that tiny variations in conditions may result in unpredictable outcomes.

In contemplating the current pandemic, some of us will also have been recalling *the law of unintended consequences*, coined by another American academic, said consequences being potentially good as well as bad, though we usually interpret it negatively.

As the world that we have known all our lives metamorphoses before our eyes; as we struggle to take in the devastation caused already and fear that which may yet be to come, there could be no more graphic example of the horrors that can come from acting before thinking, or acting without thinking at all.

The pathogen from a Chinese 'wet' market has demonstrated more conclusively than ever that wild animals are a source of danger to human beings who wish to consume them, and not just to the ones into whose system the pathogen happily passes but to millions and millions across the world who become its unwitting victims.

It is worth remembering that, albeit on a much smaller scale, how we act has its consequences, both good and bad. As the Sages said: *mitzvah goreret mitzvah, aveyra goreret aveyrah*, [M. Avot 4.2] one sensible act inspires another, but one mistake inspires another too.

15th May 202

In the book of Exodus, associated with the construction of the Tabernacle, we encounter one of the Torah's most quoted statements: God says to Moses, *ve-asu li nikdash ve-shakhanti be-tokham*, they shall build a sacred space for Me and I shall live among them [Exod.25.8]. The most frequent interpretation of this phrase is to note that God will dwell among the people once THEY have a sacred space, rather than God dwelling **in** the sacred place.

The idea that God is everywhere, a universal deity, is one that grows in the 6th century following the destruction of the Temple in Jerusalem by the Babylonians; the prophet Jeremiah writes to some of the early Judean exiles and tells them, among other things, to worship God where they are, something never said before. It was revolutionary and transformative and was the origin of Judaism. (Jeremiah 29. 1-7)

Our most common word association with 'sacred space' is probably 'synagogue', and it is the synagogue that for all our adult lives, and that of our parents, grandparents and so on, has represented the place where we have gone to worship and participate in the rites and rituals that are a key part of our self-definition as Jews.

Last year, in several conversations with members, I raised the idea of using the technology available to us, and with which I was familiar at Leo Baeck College, to do regular conversion classes, and even some teaching, in between my physical visits. It was a concept that some found deeply challenging, and I understood why – it was so alien a concept to them that they couldn't get their heads around it.

But necessity, as they say, is the mother of invention, and when the great lockdown started I knew that we had to use the available technology to reach out to people and provide what we could in our changed circumstances. I wasn't alone, all my colleagues did the same, and thus we transmuted DJPC into an online synagogue. We use Zoom, though there are other options; one of my closest colleagues chose You Tube and his synagogue now has its own channel.

I am less convinced by this because one of the greatest strengths of Zoom is that everyone who is online is there, in their little box; that may be why, apart from services, my colleague's community uses Zoom for teaching, and breakout rooms. And I am sure that Zoom has more to offer that we have not, as yet, tapped.

In spite of the easing of restrictions in some countries, and the frustration of some of their citizens that there are still any restrictions, we should remember that nothing has changed about the virus, nor will it change until a proven vaccine has been found and we all feel safe. Social distancing will continue for a very long time, and it is that, as much as anything else, that will make resuming our 'old normal' synagogue life a challenge. For now, Zoom is the new normal, and we need to make as much of it as we can.

In spite of the fact that Zoom, like all technologies, has its quirks, I actually feel very comfortable with it now, on many levels, as a vehicle for delivering as much as we can to our congregants; and as many of our members are in the vulnerable bracket through age or ill health this is their only medium for engagement.

I also find the services we do together affecting and uplifting: seeing so many on screen every week, and especially hearing people interact with each other, seeing friends wave at the screen, moves me deeply.

Zoom may not be a synagogue, it may not be 'physical' in any way, but that it is, in our use of it, spiritual is incontrovertible. Zoom may not be a Tabernacle, but we have made a sacred space of it, and I feel, in a more tangible way than I could ever have imagined, that our God is with us.

22nd May 2020

The festival of *Shavuot*, with the Ten Commandments at its heart, could be said o be the one most focused on Law. The Ten Commandments themselves are the pitomisation of the Torah, whose revelation we celebrate at *Shavuot*.

Law, *halakhah* to use its Hebrew term, is a central core of Jewish life, its study eing at the heart of a Jewish education in traditional Judaism. Yet we, as progressive ews, call ourselves post-halakhic: this means that while we may consider the *halakhah* s an important strand among many others in our Jewish culture and heritage, we do ot give it a veto on our behaviour or life-style, only a vote. We take this stand because ve do not believe that the traditional depiction of the revelation of Torah, God dictating ne words and Moses writing them down, can possibly stand any amount of stress-esting before becoming absurd.

What we do believe is that our far distant ancestors created the myths we celebrate t Shavuot to explain how the rules that governed the lives of later generations had ome about. By creating a transmission nexus between God and Moses they created a tructure which it was very hard for their contemporaries to deny.

Millennia later we can celebrate the myth, and acknowledge that even in ages past here were great sages who added to the *halakhah* when a situation occurred with which ne Torah's teachings could not deal adequately. The most famous example of this was ne action taken by no less a rabbi than Hillel himself. He considered the laws of emission of debt in the Sabbatical and Jubilee years to be disadvantageous to lenders nd borrowers alike, so he created a new structure for dealing with the situation called ne *Prozbul*, and it came to be the way for dealing with the challenge posed in this istance.

When the facts change I change my opinion, famously remarked the eminent conomist John Maynard Keynes, and that broadly seems to chime with Hillel's actions o.

When we came to transfer DJPC to the web, and become an online *kehillah edoshah*, we went through the process that has occurred in Progressive communities throughout the world. We have been doing it now for a mere 12 weeks and we have learned and will continue to learn a lot about how to do it better.

For Progressive communities this has been relatively easy, both to justify and to do, for Conservative and Orthodox Jews this is not the case. For them, a Zoom congregation, no matter how large it may be, is not a real congregation, a real minyan which means, most specifically, no *Barkhu* (not such a big deal) but also no *Kaddish* (which is about as big a deal as it gets). It also means no *shabbat* or festival services and who knows what they will do when the holiest days of the year approach.

I can't help feeling that Hillel would have found a clear way forward, creating new rules to fit the current situation. In his great halakhic masterpiece, *Mishneh Torah* in the section on Shabbat, Moses Maimonides is at pains to emphasise that the principle of *pikkuach nefesh* overrides all other laws and statutes. I would find it hard to argue that online services, instead of making people come to a confined space where they could either catch or transmit a deathly virus, was not one of the most obvious cases of *pikkuach nefesh* of which I could think. Then again, I suppose the current authorities are concerned that if they legitimized online worship on shabbat and festivals they might open the door to a whole raft of halakhah-breaking, and so for that reason they shut the possibility down.

It will be interesting to see whether and how this situation changes for them in the coming months and who knows, maybe years.

We should all be proud to be part of a Judaism that responds to the needs of the times, and especially at this time in all our lives when the boon of worship with friends and family, safely, has been made possible. In truth, Judaism has always moved with the times, and I am sure it will continue to do so. We are creating new traditions, new ways of worship, new opportunities to feel the presence of God; some perhaps will be with us far longer than we think, but all of them will strengthen and deepen our faith and our sense of what Judaism, and being Jewish, is all about.

30th May 2020

Most Jews know the name of Abraham Joshua Heschel. Most know he was a rabbi. Many know that he wrote some of the most important books on Jewish Theology and Philosophy of the 20th century. Many of them know that his writing is highly scholarly and, with a couple of exceptions, somewhat challenging. And a few know that, together with a handful of other Rabbis, Heschel marched with Martin Luther King Jr in Selma, Alabama on March 21st 1965.

But how did this all come about? What put Heschel at the forefront of a march for Black Rights?

In 1963, on January 14th, a conference was held in Chicago called "Religion and Race", and Heschel was invited to be one of the speakers. It was there he met Martin Luther King Jr., and the two became friends. In his philosophizing, Heschel often seems to practice a degree of ambiguity, giving his readers the opportunity to decide what THEY think he means. In this speech there is no holding back, his words are searing and white hot.

A couple of quotes:

Religion and race. How can the two be uttered together? To act in the spirit of religion is to unite what lies apart, to remember that humanity as a whole is God's beloved child. To act in the spirit of race is to sunder, to slash, to dismember the flesh of living humanity. Is this the way to honor a father: to torture his child? How can we hear the word "race" and feel no self-reproach?

Race as a *normative* legal or political concept is capable of expanding to formidable dimensions. A mere thought, it extends to become a way of thinking, a highway of insolence, as well as a standard of values, overriding truth, justice, beauty. As a standard of values and behavior, race operates as a comprehensive doctrine, as racism. And racism is worse than idolatry. *Racism is satanism*, unmitigated evil.

Heschel holds up a mirror to the white America of the 1960s and his words are cutting and timeless:

To some Americans the situation of the Negro, for all its stains and spots, seems fair and trim. So many revolutionary changes have taken place in the field of civil rights, so many deeds of charity are being done; so much decency radiates day and night. Our standards are modest; our sense of injustice tolerable, timid; our moral indignation impermanent; yet human violence is interminable, unbearable, permanent. The conscience builds its confines, is subject to fatigue, longs for comfort. Yet those who are hurt, and He who inhabits eternity, neither slumber nor sleep.

We who look at America ablaze following the murder of George Floyd, and who are able to strip out the criminal and political extremist elements from the demonstrations, together with the incendiary idiot living at 1600 Pennsylvania Avenue, are able to discern that the distance travelled by all of us is far, far less than we would like.

As the heirs of prophetic Judaism, which rails against injustice of any kind, we must be ready to stand up and condemn racism both verbal and physical, and to reach out in solidarity, just as Heschel did, if we are to be true to ourselves and our heritage.

Much of Heschel's speech on Religion and Race, delivered 57 years ago, could have been written yesterday, and is as much a clarion call to action now as it was all those decades ago.

What we face is a human emergency. It will require much devotion, wisdom and divine grace to eliminate that massive sense of inferiority, the creeping bitterness. It will require a high quality of imaginative sympathy, sustained cooperation both in thought and in action, by individuals as well as by institutions, to weed out memories of frustration, roots of resentment.

We must act even when inclination and vested interests would militate against equality. Human self-interest is often our Nemesis! It is the audacity of faith that redeems us.

To have faith is to be ahead of one's normal thoughts, to transcend confused motivations, to lift oneself by one's bootstraps.

Mere knowledge or belief is too feeble to be a cure of man's hostility to man, of man's tendency to fratricide. The only remedy is *personal sacrifice*: to abandon, to reject what seems dear and even plausible for the sake of the greater truth; to do more than one is ready to understand for the sake of God. Required is a breakthrough, a *leap of action*. It is the deed that will purify the heart. It is the deed that will sanctify the mind. The deed is the test, the trial, and the risk.

The way we act, the way we fail to act is a disgrace which must not go on forever. This is not a white man's world. This is not a colored man's world. It is God's world. No man has a place in this world who tries to keep another man in his place. It is time for the white man to repent. We have failed to use the avenues open to us to educate the hearts and minds of men, to identify ourselves with those who are underprivileged. But repentance is more than contrition and remorse for sins, for harms done. Repentance means a new insight, a new spirit. It also means a course of action.

Racism is an evil of tremendous power, but God's will transcends all powers. Surrender to despair is surrender to evil. It is important to feel anxiety, it is sinful to wallow in despair.

What we need is a total mobilization of heart, intelligence, and wealth for the purpose of love and justice. God is in search of man, waiting, hoping for man to do His will.

The most practical thing is not to weep but to act and to have faith in God's assistance and grace in our trying to do His will. This world, this society can be redeemed. God has a stake in our moral predicament. I cannot believe that God will be defeated.

5th June 2020

The Blackest Death

Although some scholars intriguingly choose China as the country of origin of the Black Death, it is now deemed more likely that it came from an area close to the Caspian Sea in southern Russia. Be that as it may, the plague, named centuries later as the Black Death, is reckoned to have killed 50 million people between 1346 and 1353. The bacterium responsible, *yersinia pestis*, is found in rats that live close to human habitation. It will spread through and kill all the rats it infects, which makes the rat fleas move to nearby human beings, bite them, and give them bubonic plague. Even these many centuries later, when the science is well-investigated and documented, mention of The Black Death continues to arouse a frisson of horror, and fear.

Jewish historians in the past noted that during the plague years many thousands of Jews in Europe were massacred in the towns and villages in which they lived, amid accusations of poisoning wells and causing the plague. They drew the conclusion that this butchery was carried out in response to blame for the plague levelled at the Jews. Modern historians take a different tack, and having studied contemporary documentation concluded that the reason for the brutality was not the plague but the age old one of fears stoked by the Church, financial opportunism and political interest. Be that as it may, for those defenseless Jewish communities, the outcome was the same regardless of the reasoning.

So it comes as no surprise that an unholy alliance of hardcore right wing anti Semites and anti-vaxxers have been going all out to blame the Jews, or a coalition of the US, Israel and China to depopulate the world to their advantage, for COVID-19. No doubt the bat that passed the virus to the hapless pangolin was Jewish, although of course you never know, but once again we are, in the 21st century, in the frame for plague.

Some of the neo-Nazi propaganda about this is too horrible to detail, the language they use, the infinite hatred they express, the vile cartoons, the labelling of COVID-19 as 'Jew flu' brings a chill to even the stoutest heart. So if I say think *Der Stürmer* you'll probably know what I'm talking about.

We have known for some time that in the online world, and the terrestrial one as a direct result, truth is no longer considered an absolute, merely a relative. If I believe something to be true that means it **is** true, regardless of what facts, or science, or experts say to the contrary. For the anti-vaxxers, who cover a wide spectrum, this means that vaccinations are never what they seem but are noxious substances designed to weaken and harm those that receive them for a whole range of devious reasons. Similarly, those who call Covid-19 a hoax discount film of mass graves, frantic scenes in the ICU and statistics of deaths and illness from across the world as being staged propaganda. The independent reported in late May, following research done by Oxford University, that a fifth of adults in the United Kingdom believe that COVID-19 is a hoax. That is **13,200,000** people. Heaven knows what the percentage is in the US, or France, or Italy, but it will likely be very significant.

None of this should surprise us, either as Jews or as human beings; we know on both counts the capacity of others for stupidity, brutality and self-harm. Nevertheless it should concern us. **Very much**.

These human characteristics are much on display in America at present, as the far right, encouraged by repeated dog whistles from the White House, respond to the Black Lives Matter movement. The presidential election in the States in November is going to be at the end of what I predict will be the most unpleasant, and possibly violent, campaign in US history. I am concerned by the very real prospect, as I see it, of a civil war in the States either before or after the election, especially if the current incumbent loses, but not by a significant enough margin. There will be consequences from the disregard of truth that exemplifies the current administration, and they **will** ripple out into the world to the detriment of us all.

12th June 2020

The Bigger Picture

A number of years ago, an advertising campaign was run in the UK that called itself The Bigger Picture. It had some memorable images, but the most powerful was a picture of a uniformed policeman at full throttle chasing a black criminal who was running like mad to escape arrest. Except that wasn't the whole story; the next photo to appear on the electronic hoarding was a zoom out from the original which showed the uniformed officer and his black, plain clothes colleague chasing a third man, the real criminal, as he tried to escape them.

It was simple, powerful and challenging. The Bigger Picture…

There was an interesting anniversary earlier this week, on Tuesday to be precise. On June 16th 1858, in the state house in Springfield, Illinois a thousand Republican delegates chose a man called Abraham Lincoln to be their nominee for the Senate. He gave an extraordinary nomination address, so extraordinary for its time that many saw it as the primary reason why he was not elected to the Senate.

He began by saying:

If we could first know *where* we are, and *whither* we are tending, we could then better judge *what* to do, and *how* to do it. We are now far into the *fifth* year since a policy was initiated, with the *avowed* object, and *confident* promise, of putting an end to slavery agitation. Under the operation of that policy, that agitation has not only, *not ceased*, but has *constantly augmented.* In *my* opinion it *will* not cease, until a *crisis* shall have been reached, and passed. "A house divided against itself cannot stand." I believe this government cannot endure permanently half *slave* and half *free*. I do not expect the Union to be *dissolved* -- I do not expect the house to *fall* -- but I *do* expect it will cease to be divided. It will become *all* one thing or *all* the other.

The speech indicates quite clearly the depth of the commitment to the ending of slavery that burned in Lincoln's heart, and which was ultimately to take him to the White House, a civil war and the emancipation of African and African-American slaves. The phrase, a house divided against itself cannot stand, great rhetorician though e was, is not original to Lincoln. It can be found twice in the Christian Bible, first in the Gospel of Matthew, chapter 12.24, in the King James, *And if a house be divided against itself, that house cannot stand*. The response to the police shootings in the United States of unarmed African Americans, and the demonstrations that have followed in many countries throughout the world, remind us that the legacy of the evil of slavery is still a life issue, that there are swathes of opinion which still take refuge in white supremacist delusions of superiority over those with a different skin tone.

Most especially in England, and in the States, there is a lot of atonement to do for past actions. While we may be surprised and occasionally even irritated by organisations and governments doing things as a knee jerk rather than a measured, thought through and well-presented process it is clear that however repulsed we may be by the actions of rogue policemen, we, the white population, have really no clue about the inherent racism, prejudice and disadvantage that hampers the mobility of African Americans or Afro-Caribbeans. Except of course **WE** do; we Jewish whites do know about prejudice, hatred and persecution, we **do** know how hard we have had to fight to achieve our position in society and in our careers. That is why so many rabbis and Jewish activists have given their full support to Black Lives Matter, and will doubtless continue so to do.

Lincoln's quote from Matthew's Gospel actually has a mirror image in *Pirke Avot*, the Sayings of the Sages:

Kol keneysiah she-hi leshem shamayim sofah lehitkayeym – every assembly that is dedicated to the highest principles will have lasting value, *vekhol keneysiah she-hi lo leshem shamayim sofah lo lehitkayeym*, and every assembly that is **not** dedicated to the highest principles will have no lasting value. (Avot 4.11)

Lincoln's quote from Matthew, and its Jewish equivalent, echo loud and clear down the ages, and are as true today as they ever were.

19th June 2020

You've got to accentuate...

Like many of us who have used cameras for decades, the camera we now use bears little obvious relation to the first one we ever had. I can say that with complete confidence because the first camera I had was a Kodak Box Brownie, a funny, bulky object with a tiny viewfinder. Close to 50 years later we can take high resolution pictures with our phones, and their quality is quite extraordinary.

The more serious photographers among us, however, like to have a larger range of opportunity than might be available with a mobile phone and invest in a digital camera of one kind or another. It may be a digital SLR, or a 'bridge' camera, it may be a variant on what a professional photographer friend of mine calls a PHD camera, PHD standing for Push Here Dummy.

I was bought my first digital camera in Dublin by my beloved Gilly, many years ago, it had 5 MP and I thought it was the bee's knees! Things have moved on a lot since then, and the digital SLRs that I now use have 24MP, and my good friend Mr Phillips [President of DJPC] has SLR cameras of a kind of which I can only longingly dream.

There's just one problem though; I have thousands of negatives moldering in various boxes, their content long forgotten. I know they go back to the 1980s and before, but precisely what they show is to be discovered. At least it was: but a month ago I decided to take the plunge and digitize my negatives both to preserve them and to look at them again. I knew there was a key box somewhere but I couldn't find it no matter how hard I tried. There were plenty of others so I made a start with them, and then last week, in the loft, I found the box, and ever since I have been going through them and finding pictures I am so happy to have rediscovered.

The one item of kit I needed was a scanner that would scan the negatives and transfer them to my laptop. I did my research and made the purchase and started scanning. Ultimately – I am not there yet – I will have all of my photos digitized and the most precious ones of all, of my parents particularly and of Gilly and I in our very early days will be preserved.

When I was doing my research I read a lot of things that I couldn't retell if my life depended on it, but one phrase has stuck in my mind. The photo scanner, this description said, 'takes a negative and turns it into a positive'.

Such a little phrase, yet with so many applications! It's pretty easy for a little machine to take a negative image, with all its distortions to the human eye and turn it into an image that resembles what we see and which is pleasing to behold. It's a much harder thing to do with people: by and large we would rather avoid those individuals who have a negative impact upon us than engage with them, and in truth there are 'toxic' people everywhere who are by far best left alone.

Being a positive influence, seeing the quality of redemption in others, is precisely what **we** should be to merit the reward of being deemed disciples of Aaron, of whom the Sages said 'loving peace and pursuing peace, loving your fellow human beings and bringing them to Torah'. (Avot 1.12)

There can surely be few things better than turning a negative into a positive, even if it takes some time. Bing Crosby sang a song written for him by Jonny Mercer in the 1940s, the first stanza of which went:

You've got to accentuate the positive
Eliminate the negative
Latch on to the affirmative
Don't mess with Mister In-Between

It is an essential reminder to us that we can find joy in human interaction when we identify the positives and seek the good that is in almost everyone. It also recognizes how much we would dislike it if others viewed us in the same dismissive way we all too easily see them.

26th June 2020

Keep smiling...

Shortly after the lockdown I decided that I needed to get fitter, maybe not fit, but fitter. My running and cycling days being long over the best solution seemed to be walking, albeit power walking at a fast rate. So every day since, Mottel, the larger of our two dogs, and I have been out for a very quick 40 minute walk. We have two routes the dry option, which is five minutes away from our house, is a huge field, now packed with waving golden corn, all four sides of which are set up for walkers. It is a lovely route, one side of the field abutting woods with lots of bird song and, just this week swallows flying in graceful arcs over the corn. Our wet walk is through the village on a varied route, but always including a stretch through some restored water meadows.

You see things on foot that you never see driving a car. Someone has fixed a very large poster on the back of a fence, visible from the water meadows. Its message is simple: Keep Smiling, above a large rainbow. Now Keep Smiling is a very pleasant but ultimately unachievable phrase, because no one can keep smiling. I remember trying it at the reception after our wedding and all that happened was that I had a sort of rictus grin which made my muscles ache.

It was the rainbow however which intrigued me the most. The rainbow has, since 1978, been a symbol of the LGBTQI community, demonstrating both inclusivity and diversity. So why was it chosen for the NHS? It appears to have originated at the Evelina London Children's Hospital, again as a symbol representing the inclusive nature of the hospital and the staff working within it. The pandemic, which has taken such a toll on NHS staff, then inspired children and others to draw rainbows to stick in their windows as a public sign of support for all the health workers, drawing on the rainbow's symbolization as an expression of hope in the future, of the sun returning after the rain.

The rainbow also has an older range of applications: it was used as a flag by the Co-operative movement during the 16th century German Peasants' Revolt, as a symbol of peace in Italy, as a signifier of Inca territory in Peru and Bolivia, and as the flag of the Jewish Autonomous Oblast in the early 20th century. (You'll have to look that up)

So no one can reasonably claim exclusivity in the usage of the rainbow symbol, indeed as it is seen to represent inclusivity to do so would be somewhat perverse.

Symbolic posters and banners, and especially items of clothing, be they t-shirts or lapel pins, serve several purposes: they are a source of revenue for the charities that produce them, they send out a strong message about the person wearing them, they spark a conversation about whatever the cause is (which can lead to new individuals engaging with it who weren't interested before), or they can suggest that the wearer is a poser desperate for attention.

Whatever the purpose, symbols can achieve a great deal more than the sum of their parts when worn with sincerity. Those who wear slogans simply because they think it may be cool, or good for their image, and couldn't care less about the cause itself, do a great disservice to everyone.

Being truly part of something means full engagement with it, not sloganizing; means selfless giving, means activity, means creativity, means years of commitment, means turning up. All of this applies especially to Jewish communal life, to having a community of shared faith, shared concerns and shared goals and achieving them by collaborating with each other.

A happy face and a bright image are all very well, but they are not enough. If you want to be a true supporter you have to turn up!

3rd July 2020

Shower dodging....

It's been quite a wet week here in the UK, not so much torrential more soft Irish rain, which has done wonders for our garden, and especially for my dahlias.

My daily constitutional has shifted times to get out while it was at least not raining. That is not so much because I don't like getting wet but because I live in the countryside and our dog Mottel's predominant colour is cream. So it was that, out very early on Tuesday morning, we encountered another intrepid soul with a rather battered pug, and as we passed she said to me – I see you're out dodging showers too.

One of the pleasant by-products of the pandemic (and there are precious few) has been that people are talking to each other rather than the stereotypical English behaviour of ignoring everybody when you are outside the home. So 'mornings' and 'afternoons' are now commonplace, as is 'thank you' when you socially distance from people walking towards you.

Dodging showers is quite easy to accomplish most of the time. The worst place to be is in the middle of a city where it is hard to see enough of the sky to ascertain from where rain might come or how close it is; in the countryside, where the skies are big, it isn't a problem.

Dodging COVID-19 is an altogether more daunting undertaking. For those of us who have been isolating for months the great outdoors is fraught with much more than the fear of getting wet. We are still learning about the coronavirus, SARS-CoV-2, to give it its scientific name, and what we are learning is not good, not good at all. We know the catastrophic damage it can do to the lungs, we know the devastating impact on the body of an extended period in ICU on a ventilator, we know about the fatigue and many other symptoms that are part of the virus. We know it lingers and can return. We know that it affects disproportionately people of Black and multi-ethnic origin, and we also know that it is statistically taking a severe toll of Jewish men who catch it. Above all, we know that there is as yet no provably successful vaccine, and that although there are frantic efforts to create such a vaccine these things take time.

So as I contemplate the Covidiots ignoring social distancing rules, when I think about people far too close together in shops, when I think about the drive to get people back to work in some cases in dangerous set ups where social distancing is nigh on impossible, and when I see the hordes who don't wear face masks and gloves when they are outside their homes, I am sorely troubled.

There is a wonderful saying in the *Mishnah*, Sandhedrin 4.5, that states: *whoever saves a single human life it is as if they had saved an entire world, and whoever destroys a single human life it is as if they had destroyed an entire world*. It is a dictum that has enormous resonance for us, and makes perfect sense, both in a positive and a negative way. It reminds us of our moral and ethical responsibilities to others, and also that when someone dies the impact of their demise is largely never restricted to themselves, but has a catastrophic effect on their loved ones, family and friends.

What has this to do with the virus? Everything! Our tradition teaches us that we have a duty to do nothing that endangers the life of another human being, let alone that might threaten many more. It demands that we impose discipline on ourselves, whatever the temptations, whatever the frustrations of being sequestered at home for months on end. It requires us to maintain that 2 metre distance guideline even if it changes to 1 metre. It tells us to think through government decisions and decide in whose interest they really are.

Whoever behaves thoughtlessly or recklessly and infects another human being destroys not just them but an entire world. Whoever behaves properly, who acts carefully and selflessly and thereby protects another human being, saves not just them but an entire world.

10th July 2020

Risk averse aversion….

The most famous Chinese curse, as we all know, states 'May you live in interesting times', and boy oh boy, are we living in interesting times! I imagine that, by definition, 'uninteresting' times are those in which nothing happens, but I cannot believe that 'interesting' was meant to mean **everything** happens at the same time. It seems that wherever you look dreadful things are taking place, and dreadful people wreaking havoc with impunity, and the only challenge is deciding which is worse.

Perhaps one of the things the Chinese hinted at was 'fear', and there is plenty to fear. Off the top of my head I could name 8 or 10, and with a bit of thought more, events or individuals that cause me to fear; and I say that as someone who has not consciously been aware of being afraid of anything much during my life, and for whom fear is a very new, and unwelcome, emotion.

How the world has changed! Back in the day (whatever that means) human beings did all sorts of things without a second thought. I don't mean climbing Everest, just all sorts of day to day things; walking or bussing to school, going on shopping trips, going on holiday, youth camps, and expeditions and so on. If whatever it was turned out well and was successful, we were happy; and if the opposite occurred we took it on the chin, accepted it, learned what we could from it, and moved on.

Yet, within the last 10 or 15 years, all that has changed. I remember the very first time I heard the phrase 'risk assessment': I hadn't got a clue what it was, or why it was relevant. When I found out more I could see some of the positive thinking behind it, but I was appalled by the amount of time that needed to be invested, often by more than a single person, in completing the exercise. What positive thinking? Checking out all the aspects of an endeavour to seek out potential pitfalls or difficulties so that everything might go smoothly. Benefit? A good event appreciated and enjoyed by leaders and participants alike.

So what about underlying negative thinking? Simple! Identify every aspect that could go wrong and eradicate it. Benefit? Don't get sued!

These days we hear much about being 'risk averse'; as I interpret it this refers to those who don't want to take any risks in anything they undertake. Now I'm not encouraging anyone to be reckless, but I can't help feeling that the all too easy excuse of 'risk' makes us weaker rather than stronger. It throws us on the resources of others rather than our own. It legitimizes fear: as in, No, of course I'm not afraid, I'm risk averse! And living in a time when there are many reasons to be afraid, we should be trying to strengthen our own inner resources, our will, our resolve, our sense not simply of who but <u>what</u> we are.

There's a saying in *Pirke Avot* (Sayings of the Sages, 2.5) that I have always liked: *bimkom she-eyn anashim, hishtadeyl lihyot ish*. Literally it means – in a place where there are no men strive to be a man – which doesn't really help that much. What it says, however, is much clearer: in a situation where no one does the human thing, be a *mensch*. Or, in a situation where no one else does the right thing, rise above yourself and do it.

We don't know how changed and circumscribed our lives may be in the future, but that there will be no return to the days of 2019 and before is something of which we can sadly be confident. How we respond, as creative human beings often do in the most challenging of circumstances, will dictate how we cope. The more risk averse we are, the more our lives are dictated by fear, the more our human stature, and our sense of self, will wither.

Bimkom she-eyn anashim, hishtadeyl lihyot ish.

17th July 2020

Those whom...

The A level study that I remember with the greatest fondness even after all the years that have passed, was Ancient Greek and Roman History. In the former we concentrated on the Peloponnesian Wars between Athens and Sparta, detailed in a great work of history by Thucydides. It was a brutal, drawn out conflict in the 5th century BCE, ultimately purposeless, and a saying was applied to it the authorship of which has been disputed ever since.

The saying was: *those whom the gods destroy they first make mad*. It might have been Euripides, or possibly Thucydides, or even Seneca, no one can be sure. It doesn' matter at all really, because the saying is too powerful to need a famous author, it message needs no attribution.

I have been pondering on this adage a lot in recent weeks, specifically with regard to the wearing of face masks and the response to the whole idea of compulsory mask wearing in the United States. In spite of the fact that wearing a mask lessens the likelihood of infection with COVID-19 by air borne droplets, and is also an altruistic act of protection towards their fellow citizens, there are many, hundreds of thousands who see any instruction to mask up as an infringement of their civil liberties enshrine in the Constitution.

They are, in effect, saying they would rather die from coronavirus to protect their civil liberties than wear a mask and be a responsible human being. If that isn't madness I don't know what is! Mind you, if these people are supporters of the President, the may be confused right now. This week the man who has made himself both a laughing stock and an object of utter contempt across the world has reversed his previous vehemently held position on masks and now says that wearing one is a patriotic act All one can wonder is how many thousands of lives might have been saved had he woken up to that one much, much earlier.

I remember when masks rose in profile, mainly because the NHS didn't have enough of them, saying to Gilly that face masks were going to be a huge growth industry that would make some people very, very rich. So it has happened: all sorts of companies, charities, and similar organizations have started selling face masks, from the plain to the garish, the simple to the high tech. Indeed they range from the basic to the fantastical, from what you expect to see in a hospital worn by the professionals to models on the catwalk. It is all slightly bizarre. You can actually pay as much as $500 for the most desirable ones, if you're that rich, or that stupid.

But there is an aspect to face masks that I haven't heard discussed so far and that is this. A face mask, by definition, masks the face, you can no longer see the person's mouth, or their nose. Now we might feel quite comfortable with that, an air of mystery perhaps, but there is a very negative dimension: the shape of our mouths is often the readiest reflection of our inner mood, and of our attitude to the person facing us. Hide the mouth and, unless you remove the mask itself, everyone will be kept guessing.

On a couple of occasions this week I said to a kind and smiley shop assistant, I am smiling back at you, you just can't see it! Now if, for the foreseeable future, masks, whether plain or fancy, are going to be a standard part of our dress outdoors we are going to have to find a way of compensating for the hidden mouth.

Ask almost anyone what the best kind of smile is and they will likely say ' a smile with the eyes'. You often hear it said of others, 'her smile never quite extends to her eyes'; well now the smile has to begin and continue with the eyes, and many of us have never had to practice that skill because our mouths did most of the work.

One of the Sages remarked that we should greet everyone with a cheerful face. Easier said than done a lot of the time but wise nevertheless. With masks, however, no one can tell.

So my advice this week is to start cultivating a new skill: stand in front of a mirror wearing a mask, and practice smiling with your eyes. Once you've cracked it do it, the response will warm your heart.

24th July 2020

Habla Ingles?

As the new academic year at Leo Baeck College will be taught online from September, at least for the first semester, all faculty have had to adapt their teaching accordingly. As many of you will know, bizarre thought it may be, sitting on a sofa looking at a screen is tiring; sitting and teaching is exhausting, and after too much time on screen learning most students are catatonic (so are the lecturers)! So we are all varying our modes of delivery, using what are called synchronous and asynchronous learning methods. The former means that students and lecturer are on screen together, the latter that students are learning in their own time.

An essential tool is a good digital voice recorder, and I found one such quite easily, enabling me to record introductions to classes for my modules. The little machine is tiny, simple to operate, and I am very pleased with it. One thing that did surprise me was the size of the box it came in, and the reason for that was revealed as soon as I emptied it. By far the largest component in the box was instructions for use in – Polish and Dutch, Spanish and Portuguese, Czech and Slovak, Hungarian and Romanian, Greek and Russian, Bulgarian and Slovenian. And, demonstrating that someone at SONY has a naughty sense of humour, German and Italian (can't think why they put those two together!!).

It reminded me of a well-known midrash about God revealing Torah first to Israel at Sinai, and thereafter to the 70 nations of the earth. This is, of course, a way of expressing not that the rabbis had any idea how many peoples there were on earth but rather that the language of Torah was universal, and its teachings apply to all god fearing human beings.

In the beginning, of course, the *Tanakh* tells us we all spoke the same language and this lead us to achieve such singularity of purpose that we began to build antiquity' only skyscraper. God soon put a stop to that! Well now, of course, there are many different languages, spoken by specific countries and peoples, and we for our part speak English.

The shadow of Babel's tower is a long one, however, and even though we speak the same language it often doesn't help us much. The number of times we hear simple words whose meaning we know and **misunderstand** them is a trap into which we all fall.

The most likely way to avoid misunderstandings, and the fractures that can so easily follow them, is by talking face to face and listening to each other, something my very first chairman taught me in the early 1980s, and I have followed his advice ever since. The phone is the next best way of speaking to each other, and nowadays we have WhatsApp and FaceTime which enable us to talk and see the person with whom we converse. The posted letter is the next best way to communicate because writing it takes time and you really need to think carefully about your words; in the old days there were certain letters that you 'slept on', reread in the morning and then ditched. And the worst of all ways of communicating? Altogether now... EMAIL!

The curse of email is that we can write an amazing stream of consciousness piece and press the send button before we have paused to peruse what we have written. And even when we read it through we usually just check for typos and grammar rather than looking hard at the words themselves. Emails of a practical application are normally not a problem, but anything of importance needs not just time for reflection, it needs one vital extra. We need to hear the recipient reading our words and hearing our voice as they read them, and **then** we need to reflect on what we have written.

The month of Elul has just begun, our Jewish countdown to *Rosh Hashanah*, and after a terrible year we face the prospect of something as bad if not worse in the months that lie ahead. We may find ourselves no longer in charge of our own destiny but battered by forces beyond our control. If, God forbid, such days should come we will need each other and the transcendental ties that bind us, and we should bear that in mind as we move forward and remember the true meaning of 'community'.

21st August 2020

Elbows!!!

BBC Radio 4's flagship news and current affairs programme Today began jus
over a year after I was born and it has consciously been part of my morning routine fo
over fifty years. I have listened to everyone who has presented the show, and seen tha
diversify over the decades, and also heard first broadcasts by a 'cub reporter' and thei
final broadcast when they retired. Early this week I heard a tiny bit of one story anc
particularly the following sentence: full stops in a text message are sometimes seen a
curt.

What!???, I said aloud. Anyway, I did some online research and found that thi
stems from a group of Generation Z students in the US who said they found full stop
intimidating. Generation Z are those born between 1997 and 2012 by the way, an
these sensitive souls feel that full stops indicate an abrupt or angry tone of voice.

Oy a broch, as my *bubbe* used to say. But it got me thinking about Etiquette
'polite behaviour', and how it has changed over the years. When I was growing up on
of the most grievous behaviours was putting one's elbows on the table when eating, o
indeed at any time; that and how you held a knife and fork meant that you could blen
more easily in the higher social strata to which you obviously aspired. Other points o
etiquette included speaking 'properly', giving up your seat on public transport t
someone older than yourself, opening the door for a woman (we said lady) to g
through first, and showing respect for those older than you.

These and many other issues of etiquette have faded over the intervening decade
and everything these days is much more relaxed. In some ways that may be a goo
thing, society has changed dramatically after all, in ways that could not and indee
would not have been envisaged in the 1950s; nevertheless there are still modes c
behaviour that I choose to follow because I consider them to be acts of good manner
and they, by and large, do not change.

I still hold doors open for women, or older men, rather than going through mysel
and were I suicidal enough to take public transport I would still give up my seat if
saw someone who for a range of reasons needed it more than I did. I am perfectl

comfortable with elbows on the table, though every time I do it I have the Pavlovian response hearing my father saying 'Elbows' in a slightly menacing tone!

The closest analogy to 'good manners' in Hebrew is '*derekh eretz*' (which my spellchecker replaced with 'Derek erects', somewhat disrupting my train of thought). Literally that means 'the way of the land' but in its applied sense it covers respect, decency, concern for other people and an ability not to put oneself at the centre of everything.

Samson Raphael Hirsch, a 19th century German rabbi and creator of modern Orthodox Judaism, called his movement '*Torah im Derekh Eretz*', a phrase that I have always liked and found very meaningful. To me, *Torah im derekh eretz* is not just a description but an instruction to those who lead and those who teach. There is no point in teaching something and despising those you teach; there is no point in being learned if you use your learning to humiliate other people who know less; there is no point in being overtly pious if behind closed doors you are anything but; there is no point in knowing everything about *halakhah* if you uncaringly allow it to hamper and disadvantage the life of others.

Torah im derekh eretz as it applies to all of us is an excellent mantra and guide to how we should live our lives. It means showing respect to all; it means common decency; it means putting concern for others over concern for yourself; it means learning and putting that learning to good effect - in our homes, our relationships and our world.

28th August 2020

The Final Frontier?

Space, the final frontier, these are... NOT the voyages of the Star Ship Enterprise this is the first of my four sermons for the Yamim Noraim in 2020.

On July 25th 1970, at precisely 02.56AM UK time, Neil Armstrong set foot on the moon and took a 'giant leap for mankind'. I watched it live, with my parents, in my room in a Bournemouth hotel; the picture was grainy but it was still incredible Reflecting back on this event of 51 years ago, I think it safe to say that the Apollo project, culminating in the landing of the Eagle lunar module on the moon's surface changed the world forever. If that sounds like hyperbole it is worth clarifying that NASA did much more than build rockets, it initiated programmes which led to many of the modern information and communication technologies that we take for granted in our everyday lives. Many of these feats of micro-engineering continue to reverberate; I remember when the first Personal Computers appeared, the first mobile phones, the internet, smart phones, ipods etc., without which the life of hundreds of millions of people would be immeasurably poorer. There is a linear progression from the space missions of NASA to the iPhone and we need to remind ourselves at times that it is not the boffins at Apple HQ that deserve all the credit, much of it we owe to thousands of unnamed and unknown specialists working in Texas and Florida who creating extraordinary machines that had never existed before.

There are few events of which it can be safely said that they change the world; we all know that the Coronavirus pandemic is not just one such, but that it is highly likely that for many the lives we lead up to March 2020, and the lives we have lead and will continue to lead since, mark one of the most profound such shifts in modern human history.

At this time of reflection, particularly this year, we can reflect on 12 months that have passed like no other; the year between last Rosh Hashanah and the March 2020 lockdown, and between the latter and today. If we think hard of the catastrophic pandemic whose iron grip on the world continues, we cannot but feel dismay and disbelief in almost equal measure.

There is still something so surreal, so incredible – in the truest meaning of that word – and so distressing about COVID-19; and the fact that we have no idea whatsoever about the future and its impact on our countries and societies, makes these emotions even harder to bear.

We have recited a *she-he-cheyanu* after each erev Shabbat service since lockdown because that prayer has taken on a new meaning in the Covid 19 world. We are not just saying it's lovely to share a *simchah*, we're expressing gratitude for simply being alive. Other prayers and texts speak to us in a more graphic way than they have before because we are living in such dreadful and unprecedented times.

The process of *teshuvah*, of repentance, takes on added meaning this year too. *Teshuvah* literally means 'returning' and it is undoubtedly the case that many of us have been returning to a way of living that was diminishing pre-pandemic. For many, home was a place you slept and had a few meals in, but you probably spent much more time outside it. All that has changed: eating in is the new eating out, Amazon Prime, Netflix and Disney + are the new going to the movies, working from home is the new working, and for many of us that is just fine.

Equally, our faith communities have seen far greater levels of virtual engagement than they used to of a physical kind; the practices and ideas that many had a passing or peripheral relationship with are now more central to the existence of many. Not just a way of reaching out to others but also a way of reaching in, a way of reaching towards God.

Reflecting on the last year we are painfully aware of the many errors and mistakes by our leaders, as well as of the increasingly fascistic tendencies of some world leaders which are threatening to everyone. We are probably less comfortable, less confident, than at any time since the Second World War, and no easy relief is in sight.

When he launched the US space mission to the Moon, President Jack Kennedy told America: we do these things not because they are easy but because they are hard.

It is the same with us: over these 10 days particularly we do the hard things: reflection, self-analysis, self-criticism.

In many ways it doesn't get much harder than this, but our tradition DEMANDS it of us. And this year we do not just contemplate ourselves; we reflect on our world and what has brought us to this point, and we must, we truly must, commit to trying in some way, to rebuild it.

Erev Rosh Hashanah 572
17th September 202

A mirror on the universe

In 1990 the Space Shuttle Discovery launched the Hubble Telescope into a low earth orbit. Circling the globe above rain clouds, light pollution and atmospheric distortion, it has gifted humanity with unforgettable pictures of distant stars and galaxies as well as the planets in our solar system.

At its launch, Hubble was the most sophisticated telescope ever made, and over the thirty years since its launch it has had many of its systems updated, extending its life and ensuring it remains at the cutting edge. The statistics are incredible: in its lifetime Hubble has made more than 1.4 million observations and provided material for over 17,000 peer reviewed scientific papers. It has watched a comet collide with Jupiter, discovered moons around Pluto, found star nurseries in the Milky Way and discovered space phenomena 13.4 billion light years from earth.

The science and statistics are amazing enough, but the photographs? They are awe-inspiring, beautiful, uplifting and a potent reminder of the smallness of Planet Earth in the vastness of space, and the minuteness of humanity.

On a day which the rabbis also called the Birthday of the World, however, we direct our attention not to the skies but to that most parochial and yet enthralling microcosmos, the dysfunctional human family. The story of the *Akeydah*, the Binding of Isaac, is supposed to be about faith, that was certainly how the majority of the Sages interpreted it; the *Akeydah* was the tenth and final test of Abraham's faith, set by God, and the Patriarch came through it with flying colours, as he had in the previous nine.

Yet scrutiny with a modern eye of this famous story and the texts just before and just after it draw us to a different focus. Abraham and Sarah have a very long relationship, and it sees them through a lot; but it remains childless for years until Sarah agrees that her servant, Hagar, may have a child from Abraham.

However bitter a pill her initial agreement may have been is nothing compared to the anger and jealousy that she feels after a son is born to Hagar, Ishmael. Once Isaac is born Sarah turns her resentment on Hagar and Ishmael and has them kicked out of Abraham's encampment. Abraham doesn't argue with his wife, and God reassures him that all will be well, but he is clearly upset, if not even angry with Sarah for putting him in this position.

This anger is practically expressed in the manner of his departure from his own camp with Isaac. He steals away with his son and a couple of servants early in the morning and deprives Sarah of the chance to say goodbye to her only child. With fractured relations between husband and wife we can imagine the mixture of rage and grief when she discovered that Abraham and **her** son had disappeared, no one knowing where they had gone or when they would return.

We all know how hard it is to maintain family relationships. Hard because they require constant engagement and constant effort; hard because they often fall victim to circumstances beyond people's control; hard because misunderstanding can lead to mistrust, and without trust the core, the bedrock of human relationships, those relationships will founder and fail.

There is a wonderful phrase in the book of Proverbs, the only biblical book in which it is found, and which always amused me when I was a child. The phrase is *Chadrey-veten* or *va-ten. Cheder* means room and *Beten* means womb, so the phrase means The Rooms of the Womb, which is why, I guess, I found it funny. Look up the translations and apart from the King James Bible which renders as 'the innermost part of the belly', the standard rendition is 'innermost parts of the body', which could perhaps be more poetically translated as 'the deepest parts of our being'.

Is it not ironic that humanity has had the wherewithal to send the mightiest of machines into deep space yet the route to understanding our innermost feelings and motivations still eludes us? So often do we inflict unwonted suffering on others because we fail to understand ourselves, or because we prioritise our own needs over those of others, or because we thought too highly of ourselves and too little of others.

These are the thoughts we should have at this penitential season, and if we use it well we will find our way to a better life, more in harmony with others and at peace with ourselves.

The photographs of deep space from Hubble were and remain awe-inspiring as well as beautiful; yet there is nothing out in space more beautiful than human beings ere on earth who truly understand themselves, warts and all, and through that self-nowledge build strong and constructive relations with each other for the betterment f all. Our human future on the grandest and smallest scale depends on us getting this ght. We <u>must</u> not, we <u>cannot,</u> fail.

Rosh Hashanah Shacharit 5721

18th September 2020

Kol Nidrey 2020

In August 2018 NASA launched arguably its greatest mission, the Parker Solar probe. It is the first space mission whose focus is not a planet, but a star, to whit, the Sun. The facts and statistics are extraordinary: it is the fastest machine created by human beings, travelling at an almost incomprehensible 450,000 miles an hour. In journeying to the sun the intention is to fly it into the sun's atmosphere and learn as much as we can from that proximity. It is now some 29,312,048 miles from the earth and when it enters the sun's atmosphere it will still be some 4 million miles from the sun's surface.

NASA makes it clear that the subtext of the project is not just science for its own sake, but also to try and understand aspects of the sun and of Earth's space environment that affect life and society. It is an immense aspiration, an extraordinary feat of human engineering, and a reminder in this fractured world of ours that human beings can achieve miracles when they work together.

In many ways *Kol Nidrey* is the most important part of *Yom Kippur*. The solemnity of the service begins at the very start, when *Kol Nidrey* itself, a legal text of ancient lineage, is chanted or read. Nothing like this occurs at any other time in the year, as the *sifrey torah* form a ceremonial *Beit Din* and we all stand for judgement. This moment breaks the liturgical harmony of the entire year, it imposes itself between what came before and what comes after, it is like the echo from a mighty gong which continues to reverberate for some time after it has been struck.

We fail to appreciate this, we fail to derive this meaning, often because we fail to understand the purpose of the *Yamim Noraim* themselves. The Days of Awe are not just about saying sorry to God for the things we have done wrong in our lives, or the Jewish things we have failed to do, God knows them all anyway. Nor are the Days of Awe about saying sorry for the things we have done to other people. The Days of Awe are about something much, much more. We are duty bound to do the small stuff, both to God and to people, but the real purpose and meaning of the Days of Awe, which culminate tomorrow with *Yom Kippur*, is all about you, and me, about each of us.

Life as most of us live it is full of challenges: it may be getting up in the morning, washing and preparing our bodies for a new day; it may just be getting out of bed; it may be going to work and sitting in an office full of people you either don't like or with whom you have nothing in common; it may be the job you do which remunerates you only with money; it may be the decision to break free from whatever you feel constrains you; it may mean dealing with failing health. Whatever it may be, these challenges are both real and debilitating, and whether it's one of the ones I have listed or others, we all have them. Life as most of us live it is full of contradictions: it may be telling our children how they ought to behave and doing the opposite ourselves; it may be proclaiming the importance of the law, then speeding in our cars or cheating on our tax returns; it may be talking climate change in public and doing nothing about reducing it in private; it may be fulminating about animal cruelty and then giving our own animal companions less attention than they deserve; it may be talking about the importance of honesty in others and shading the truth in our own domain; whatever it may be, these challenges are both real and debilitating, and whether it's one of the ones I have listed or others, they are common to us all.

When there is a partial or full eclipse of the sun, it draws in millions of people across the world. Every time this occurs we are advised not to look directly at the sun, regardless of the degree of eclipse, because it will damage our eyes, and those who take the advice seriously will bring with them a variety of contraptions to protect their vision. Who knows what pictures the Parker Solar Probe will beam back to us, but I imagine that the heat and brilliant light will put it under great strain.

On this night, this break in time and space, the light of God beams down to us with the brilliance of a thousand suns, illuminating our secrets and secret places. Our determination to change for the better, our commitment to self-improvement, our ability to self-scrutinize successfully, will define not just how we will stand in 12 months' time before God at *Kol Nidrey*, but the positive difference we have made to our relationships with others, and with the world.

Kol Nidrey 5721

28th October 2020

The Red Planet

Of all the planets in the solar system, few have exerted a pull on the imagination of human beings over the millennia more than Mars, the Red Planet. Mars is 4,217 miles in diameter, 128 million miles from the Sun, and 35 million miles from earth. A day on Mars is 24.6 hours and it takes 1.88 years to orbit the sun. And the temperature on the planet is -65 degrees C, which I would not exactly label 'comfortable'.

Mars has been the source of countless stories, has inspired music and art, and is the planet that is the closest to earth and an obvious choice for the next big space mission. So after some robot landings over the last few years, NASA launched the Perseverance Rover Mission on July 30th 2020. If you go on the NASA website you can see how it is doing; at the time of writing this it had traveled just over 72,000 miles at a speed of 69 thousand mph. It still has 220,000 miles to travel to reach Mars. Perseverance is due to land on Mars on February 18th 2021, in the Jezero Crater, and be on the surface for 687 days, equivalent to a Martian year.

This is but the latest human endeavour to try and answer the long-standing question about whether it would one day be possible for human beings to live on Mars. Of course, there will likely be a manned landing at some point in the next 10-20 years, but even if the erection of structures safe for human beings to live in were possible it doesn't sound like much fun.

Human achievements like this are symbolic of human determination, creativity, vision and resolve, to name but four, and on one level at least we can express our admiration, wonder, even awe. And yet, I'm afraid I can't help thinking, what's the point? Why colonise space when we can't manage life on earth? Why channel human ingenuity into an out of this world project than a down to earth project right here?

If we have learned one thing in a year full of uncomfortable truths, it is that humanity is at grave risk. Though distracted by COVID-19 in all its terrible permutations, the environmental backdrop is getting steadily worse.

The catastrophic fires in the Americas, in Australia, Africa and elsewhere; the rising temperatures and droughts; the rapidly melting Antarctic ice sheets, the lack of ce in the Arctic; tundra fires in Russia which are burning off the permafrost that has or millennia contained vast quantities of methane that are now pouring into the eavens, exponentially increasing global warming; the devastating collapse of myriads of species of insect, reptile, bird and mammal; rising sea temperatures that make ever more devastating hurricanes more frequent; the catastrophic deforestation in the Amazon and in the Pacific region; all of them pose a considerable threat to humanity.

We spend a lot of time during the penitential season talking about matters of the mind and the spirit. We contemplate our moral life and always find ourselves wanting. In addition, this year, we have the added stress of coronavirus, of growing totalitarianism in Europe and America, and the rise of the Far Right.

There is so much it is hard to know what to think about first.

We have to start with ourselves, however, regardless of everything else. We have to start with accepting that in the 21st century our tradition demands of us that we explicitly do not turn inwards but see fulfilling the best of our faith in our engagement with the world. We have to acknowledge our responsibility to do whatever we can to save the planet; remember our Sages saying that whoever saves a single human life saves an entire world? Well, turn that round and say, whoever works to save the world works to save all life on earth.

Don't spend your time on this holy day just thinking about all the usual things, the traditional themes associated with the penitential season, raise your eyes to a farther horizon. Travelling to the Red Planet in the cause of science is fine, but we have a much harder task to engage with on the Blue Planet, our world. That needs to be the overarching message for us as Jews, today, tomorrow, and every day thereafter.

Yom Kippur 5721
29th October 2020

Threats

Ireland went into a full lockdown a few days before England did last March. A your Rabbi Emeritus and working with the then leadership of the congregation, w decided to embrace Zoom and on the first post-lockdown Shabbat I led the service and have been doing so ever since. One of the first challenges was thinking abou sermons, as imposing a 12-15 minute standard synagogue sermon on people watchin online seemed to me to be both unfeeling and unnecessary.

So I took the decision to restrict myself to 750 words MAX, just over 5 minutes on the grounds that it was a good discipline to work under, and, if I couldn't sa something meaningful in 6 ½ minutes I probably couldn't say it in 15!

The US Presidential election, the outcome of which is still undecided, always ha the potential to accentuate the *Mar* in *Marcheshvan*: the prospect of four more years o POTUS 45 a profoundly bitter pill for so many to force down their throats. We know of course, that the ultimate decision is not ours to make, and that a final decision ma yet be some way away. But we know that the decision will have a profound impact o us, and the entire world.

Instability in America for the next four years, following the last four, with th growing menace of right wing nationalism in the States and many other countries, wit the vital need to co-operate internationally over an effective vaccine for COVID-1 with the climate emergency deepening across the world with every day of inaction, th capacity for unlimited chaos and catastrophe could be exponential.

One of my favourite parts of *parashat Vayeyra* comes near the beginning, whe three men, (or maybe they are angels), tell Abraham's post-menopausal and aged wi Sarah that she will bear a son. But it is not her hilarity and earthy response that I cheris but rather the little phrase…

…*Chadal lih-yot le-Sarah orach nashim*, demurely translated as 'it had ceased t be with Sarah after the manner of women'.

We are aware when significant changes occur in our personal lives; everyone i a family sees each other growing up, growing older, and growing old. All we need fc hat is to take note of birthdays, and, if we are so blessed, wedding anniversaries. What s less easy to identify is change in society, particularly as it affects our civil liberties, he nature of our democracy; insidious change like a malevolent spirit wafts around us, ut we do not really see it until something strikes us and we then realise what has ccurred. We are disbelieving – how did that happen?, we ask. And the answer is – we weren't paying sufficient attention.

The last four years have echoed to the sound of warning sirens, telling us to wake up, to take note, and then to act.

But submerged by Brexit, distracted by Trump, depressed by COVID-driven ockdowns and economic uncertainty, we have waved them away, they were all just oo much: let someone else take up the struggle, let someone else stick their head above he parapet…I no longer have the energy. And so it happened, *chadal lihyot*, it had eased to be.

Chadal lihyot, it had ceased to be: in our flight away from the enormities around s, too many things have ceased to be, too much has been twisted, perverted, cankered, nd we have uttered not a word. *Chadal lihyot*, it had ceased to be - no moral leadership, he corruption of the political process, the insidious demolition of great offices of state, nd great servants of the state, the ever clearing path to autocracy, to dictatorship.

Chadal lihyot, it had ceased to be: optimism, belief in ourselves, belief in a future or our children and grandchildren. *Chadal lihyot*, it had ceased to be.

And we did nothing.

6th November 2020

Black lives matter

In southern India, in the Karnataka region, there is a wildlife sanctuary called Kabini. It is an area rich in the panoply of glorious wildlife that is India's heritage including some of the biggest tuskers on the sub-continent, massive elephant bulls with tusks over 2 metres long.

But it was something else that caught my eye on one of the photo feeds I follow a jet black leopard. Like a dark wraith in the jungle, its deep yellow eyes the only feature in a different colour, it shone like obsidian against a lush green background.

Black leopards, often called black panthers, are the colour they are for a reason science calls them melanistic. Melanism is the term for an excessive amount of black pigment in the fur. Sometimes it is very strong and other times it is weaker, but in all cases if the light is right the rosettes that we associate with a leopard's fur may still be seen.

Melanism is not the sole preserve of leopards, it is found in other big cats particularly jaguars, the equivalent of Asiatic and African leopards in the Americas. The cause of melanism is a recessive allele (each of two or more alternative forms of a gene that arise by mutation and are found at the same place on a chromosome) in leopards and a dominant one in jaguars.

Once I started following the leopard I discovered that he had a female who was the standard leopard colour, and many fabulous photos have been taken of them particularly mating on the branch of a massive tree.

Around the time that George Floyd was murdered I was also sent footage of a melanistic male jaguar called Neron, who had been introduced to a 'normal' colour female jaguar called Keira. I have rarely been so moved by watching these two powerful big cats who almost immediately fell in love. How do I know? Because there was not just an absence of tension when they met they were all over each other, and not as a prelude to mating, just because the attraction and affection was instant. It was such a powerful metaphor as the black lives matter campaign got underway, and shared the footage with all those I knew would immediately understand the message.

A year or so ago, another amazing image appeared on Instagram: this time of a ebra foal in the Serengeti in Africa. Instead of being black and white striped it was rown all over with cream polka dots. A lion'll have that was my first, pessimistic hought, but the foal, named Tira, has survived. Go and search for her if you are nterested, you'll be amazed by how she looks; and if you search a little longer you'll ind photos of her with her mother, surrounded by a herd, all of whom have clearly ccepted her as one of them.

The Racial Inclusivity in the Jewish Community report, written for the Board f Deputies by Stephen Bush and published in April, made for some grim reading. We ews, victims of an enduring and vicious form of racism we call anti-Semitism are owhere near as racially sensitive as our history suggests we should be. There may be wer black and BAME Jews in the Jewish community of these islands than in merica, but we don't seem to make them as welcome as we should. Anyone coming a synagogue who doesn't look like *unserer* can, it seems, be treated with suspicion d even unpleasantness.

All of us struggle with our own prejudice, it seems to be an unavoidable part of e human condition; but if everyone should strive to rise above their own unworthier oughts, that duty rests doubly on our shoulders. I urge you to read the report online d ponder its implications.

What happened to the jaguar lovers, Keira and Neron? They are as inseparable as er but two became three on the 6th of April, with the birth of a gorgeous blue eyed b called Inka.

Oh yes, in case you're wondering, Inka is black!

9th July 2021

In plain sight…

During a tutorial this week with one of the final year students, whose dissertation I am supervising, the subject of transliteration came up. Transliteration is the word used for writing the letters of one language in the letters of another.

The transliteration with which I am the most familiar is from Hebrew, the purpose being to help people who can't read Hebrew yet nevertheless wish to join in with the recitation of Hebrew prayers. The use of transliteration in *Siddur Lev Chadash* was vetoed at the time, but when Andrew Goldstein and I edited *Machzor Ruach Chadashah* we took the decision to include transliterated prayers, and today the use of transliteration in Jewish prayerbooks is widely present, regardless of denomination.

Ah, but what system do you use? Because I'm afraid to say that there are a number! For purists, the transliteration or Romanization of Hebrew that is *primus inter pares* is that of the Academy of the Hebrew Language, a body established in 1953 specifically to be the "supreme institution for scholarship on the Hebrew language". But there are others, and nothing to stop anyone weighing in with one of their own. For me the over-riding consideration is simplicity and ease of reading and hopefully the work I did on this for the machzor has helped some worshippers to engage with worship at the same time as their fellows, rather than being restricted to the English translation of prayers.

The main thrust of the conversation with the student concerned gutturals, particularly the letters *chet* and *khaf*. When we teach people Hebrew for the first time we tell them that both letters should be pronounced as 'ch', like 'loch'. Now 'loch' is spelt with a CH, so it is completely understandable if those new to Hebrew fix in their minds that both letters are spelt by the same two letters.

For Hebraists the two letters are distinct, the *chet* being transliterated with a *c* and the *khaf* with a *kh*. If you know Hebrew and share something transliterated with another scholar it will stick out a mile if you miss-transliterate *chet* or *khaf*, and they will wonder whether your knowledge of Hebrew is that sound.

The Torah portion for this week, which kicks off the saga of Abraham and his descendants, starts with two words that are probably the best known occurrence of *Khaf - Lekh Lekha*, spelt '*l e k h l e k h a*'.

Apart from their transliteration these two words have a depth of meaning that may not at first be apparent. Literally the words mean 'go to yourself' but as the context is one of a long journey that hardly makes sense. 'Go forth' is how the JPS Tanakh translates, and the New Revised Standard Version just says 'go'. In his monumental translation of the entire Tanakh Professor Robert Alter uses 'Go forth' but in a note makes a very interesting point. He says that before this moment Avram (as he then was) was merely part of a wave of migration across the Fertile Crescent; at this moment Avram is singled out by God and becomes an individual from whom an extraordinary history will unfold.

The Zohar, the *ur*-text for Jewish mysticism, has no problem with *Lekh lekha*, meaning 'go to yourself'. In Bereyshit 1.78a it interprets the two words as meaning 'go for yourself, fulfil yourself, reach your potential'.

This is something with which many of us can empathize: before embarking on any major venture we need to know ourselves, our capacity and capability, even if our changing circumstances bring out incredible qualities and inner strength of which we did not know we were capable. God is saying three things to Avram with the two word command *Lekh lekha*: first, that he has a task to fulfil, second that he needs to engage in inner as well as outer preparation, and third that God has confidence that he will rise to whatever challenges lie ahead of him and overcome them.

Two little words, correctly transliterated or not, that mean so much, and continue to do so. Know yourself, your strengths and weaknesses, before you take a major step, and be open not just to the trials that face you but to the innate ability and inner strength with which you will triumph over them.

October 15th 2021

Prayer for the Year

Almighty God~

12 months since our last 'lockdown *Yamim Noraim*' we gather again together with each other, albeit still in our own homes.

As we begin a process of reflection during these Days of Awe we think of those we have lost to the pandemic in the past year, as well as those who survived Covid 19 but carry long Covid with them into a future blighted by ill health and physical frailty.

We think also of the ways in which our nations have been lead during this extended crisis; many individuals have acted selflessly, courageously and correctly, many politicians far less so. We reflect with gratitude on the scientific genius that has created Covid-19 vaccines, which have helped many to feel more confident about the future, and we acknowledge that in the long struggle against Covid, and the mutations that will inevitably erupt, we will again have need of their best efforts to keep as many of us as safe as possible.

We think of the events that have taken place during this year: in a year dominated by tragedy across the world we are grateful for the lighter moments like the Tokyo Olympics, which have distracted us from our travails, and those that have added to our darkness, quintessentially the catastrophe in Afghanistan. Most serious of all, in the long term, we reflect on the countless, terrible examples throughout the world of climate change and global warming, and their effect on our weather and well-being. The heat domes, the tundra fires, the flash flooding and extreme rainfalls, the melting ice sheets, the ice free Arctic – these are humanity's outcomes for treating the planet as if it was an infinite cornucopia.

We think of those men and women who have shown fathomless compassion and care to others, doctors, nurses and therapists at the frontline of the pandemic, many of whom gave their lives for their patients. And we ask ourselves: have we done anything heroic over the last year? Have we done anything out of altruism, generosity and compassion, or have we given those responsibilities to others and shirked them ourselves?

At this service, on the eve of the new year, we unravel our flaws and failings in our sight, Eternal One, relying on your lovingkindness to forgive our wrongdoings, ur selfishness, our closed minds.

Inspire us to be greater than ourselves in the year to come; encourage us to reach ut to others; help us to understand that the deepest human fulfillment is to be found ι caring for our fellow men and women.

And support us, Eternal, as we struggle with hope and fear and tumult; strengthen s with your light, and gift us with purpose.

Keyn yehi ratzon, may this be God's will.

Rosh Hashanah 5782

6th September 2021

Generational Shift

On average, in at least the first 18-20 years of our existence, we tend to be known to others through our parents... *ah, yes, you're so-and so's son or daughter.* Post 20 and especially when we begin to build a career and make a name for ourselves everything changes round and it becomes... *ah, yes, you're so-and so's parents,* often plus... *you must be very proud.*

When parents take the wrong path in life, or make choices which affect their children negatively, the parents get castigated and the children get sympathy. When children go off the rails they may be sympathized with but the parents get castigated. Phrases like... *the apple doesn't fall far from the tree,* and *is it any wonder considering her father/mother/parents...* are often uttered.

The traditional *haftarah* for the first day of *Rosh Hashanah* is taken from Samuel which describes the birth of the last judge and first prophet, Samuel. Mirroring the miraculous birth of Abraham and Sarah's son Isaac, it tells the story of the birth of a son to Hannah, the long barren wife of Elkanah, who becomes pregnant after transactionally praying to God with great fervour at the Temple in Shiloh. I say transactionally because that is the nature of her prayer; effectively she bargains with God saying – You give me a son and I will dedicate him to you.

When said son is born and named Samuel, once he is weaned she takes him and several sacrificial offerings with great ceremony to Shiloh and then leaves him in the care of Eli, the chief priest. Intriguingly, she has changed her language since making her original vow. Then she said she would dedicate him to God, now she says, and says it twice, that she will lend him to God, which is quite different.

As a child was weaned at anytime between 18 months and 5 years, Samuel was a little boy when his mother abandoned him into the care of an old man he had never met and in a place to which he had never been. We get diverted from this by the drama of the story and Hannah's faith, and fail to appreciate the uncomfortable details that are also present.

Samuel may never have interacted with his mother again, the text doesn't mention it; he grows up in the Temple, God speaks to him and he gradually grows in stature. Eli dies, and his sons, who were corrupt priests, are killed in battle by the Philistines. Samuel too has sons who go bad, neglected, one suspects, by their father.

The adult Samuel is a huge figure in the early history of Israel. He keeps the tribes on the straight and narrow, he is their conduit to God and vice versa, he is their leader.

When the people want a king to lead them rather than Samuel, the prophet acts like a jealous child, insulted by their request even though he ultimately agrees to it; and when King Saul is anointed, Samuel's relationship with him is prickly at best, and petulantly unhelpful at worst.

We often fail to see, or even look for, anything that is present but beneath the surface; it is far easier to be impressed by someone than it is to consider the impact their fame, success, piety may have on their children. If Isaac and Samuel are anything to go by, the devotion to God of their father and mother respectively did them great damage.

Indeed it is often the case that those who profess a great love of God do not reflect that love for human beings; that is people in general, and their families in particular. After all, if God occupies all your available space how can there be room for anyone or anything else?

During these days of awe, let us reflect on our own human relationships, starting with our families but eddying outwards: have we given them the love they deserved or needed, have we shown kindness and consideration, have we made the effort to reach out to strangers in dire need, or have we kept our eyes down and our hearts closed?

This may not be the predictable grand theme of the high holy days, but if we seek forgiveness from God it is with an honest appraisal of our human relationships that we must begin, and if necessary improve. This matters even more since the pandemic changed all our lives, and we must mend what is damaged or broken, if we are to feel God's forgiving love.

Rosh Hashanah 5782
7th September 2021

Turn, turn, turn or plus ça change

The conjugation system in biblical Hebrew verbs is based on three root letters. So, for example, the root of the word *kedushah*, holiness, is *kuph dalet shin*. Some roots have weaker letters, or gutturals like *chet* in them, and as verbs they can ostensibly do strange things. The root *shuv*, from which *shuvah* is derived, is known as an *Ayin Vav* verb, because its middle letter is a *Vav*, and as a consonant that is also a vowel it does interesting things as it conjugates.

The root *Shuv* means to return, hence *Shabbat shuvah*, the Sabbath of Returning. And the noun *teshuvah* has the applied meaning of repentance, though the actual meaning is turning back or desisting from. When I was pondering this yesterday something I had never thought of before came into my mind, all of it predicated on the weak second root letter.

Today is the 20th anniversary of the Al Qaeda terror attacks on the United States. All of us alive at the time will remember where we were when we first heard the news, and indeed when we saw the truly horrific film of the aircraft crashing into the twin towers. There were many other images we saw that will live with us forever, the man jumping to his death rather than stay in the building, the massive dust cloud that enveloped everybody and everything as the skyscrapers fell to earth and much more.

2,996 people died on 9/11 and more than 6000 people were injured. Between then and now more than 125,000 people have enrolled on the WTC Health programme and 18,000 have suffered cancer that is 9/11 related.

President George W Bush declared a war on terror in the immediate aftermath and shortly thereafter attacked Afghanistan, the state which had given Osama bin Laden refuge and a base from which he could launch his outrages. Since 9/11 some 929,000 people have died in the war on terror, some 390,000 non-combatants have been killed, 38 million people have been displaced, and the price tag for the US alone is 8 trillion dollars.

One of the most important Jewish actions is that of *teshuvah*, repentance; as the *machzor* liturgy says *u-teshuvah u-tefillah u-tzedakah ma-avirin et ro-a ha-gezeyrah*, and repentance, prayer and righteous acts diminish the severity of the judgement. And we should note that *teshuvah* comes first....

Yet *teshuvah* comes from a root with a vowel letter in its core, a weakness, and *teshuvah* has that same weak little vowel/consonant; to me that is a reminder of the inherent weakness in this whole process, the flaw that our humanity grants us, that we are slow to change, that we learn nothing from the mistakes we have made in the past, that our inclination is always to blame others rather than being honest with ourselves.

And however serious that may be for us as individuals, when the scope is national or international it can be catastrophic.

On September 11th 2001, the biggest attack on the USA since Pearl Harbor was perpetrated. It was a second day of infamy. In response, barely a month later, America carpet bombed the Tora Bora mountains in Afghanistan and on the 19th of October US ground forces entered the fray. The flaw in the endeavour was a failure to learn the lessons of history; no armies since Alexander the Great have ever successfully subjugated Afghanistan, the British Empire failed, so did the Soviet Union, and so have the Americans.

It can all be summarized in one sentence, as grim a proof of the policy and tactical weakness as you could get: in 2001 a fundamentalist Taliban regime, supported Al Qaeda in its midst while it attacked America and changed the world. In 2021, precisely twenty years since that original atrocity, and in spite of the money and the lives lost and blighted, a fundamentalist Taliban regime is in control of Afghanistan once more and has welcomed Al Qaeda into its midst.

Plus ca change, plus c'est la meme chose.

Shabbat Shuvah 5782
11th September 2021

Taking Stock

The phrase '*taking stock*' is first attested in 1510 with regard to the moving of cattle from a farm; it crops up in a theatrical context in 1761, and from 1870 it is used as we would use it, *to regard as important, to give serious consideration to...* and *to make an appraisal of something.* If we never do it at any other time of the year, *Kol Nidrei* is the moment when we do; we take stock of all the things that are important to us: loved ones, careers, friends, attitudes, actions and so on. There are also the religious elements from our tradition, regardless of our Jewish affiliation: acknowledging our sins against God, and each other; taking responsibility for the things we have done wrong and the good we failed to do.

Many years past I remember how as a young rabbi it was these themes that were expected to be the grist of every sermon over the High Holy Days; fail to include them and you would be asked why. Yet in more recent times these abiding themes of the *Yamim Noraim* seem to have lost their immediacy. Who is to blame for this evolution in Jewish life? To be fair I think it is all of us, rabbis and laity alike. After all, we influence each other, and share our concerns and preoccupations, so it is hardly surprising. And in the past eighteen months or so, as much as connecting with each other on a Jewish basis has grown exponentially, so too the cares and obsessions which have plagued us during the pandemic have taken us in our minds and hearts to other issues, chief among them global warming and climate change.

As catastrophic event after catastrophic event has occurred across the world, the slowing of the gulf stream, the shrinkage of the Greenland ice sheet, the absence of ice in the Arctic Ocean in the summer, massive rainfall and terrible flooding, droughts and searing temperatures, wildfires on all continents, even more deadly hurricanes, it is hard to blot these things out and think of other matters. There has been little doubt in my mind for many years that climate change posed the biggest existential threat to the planet, and thereby also to humanity, and all of the creatures that we haven't yet persecuted or hunted to extinction. But how does that fit with the *Yamim Noraim*, the Days of Awe?

We know that the ancients were keen observers of the natural world from the range of creatures listed in the dietary laws as permissible or forbidden for consumption; we know that there was an appreciation of the agricultural economy from the *Bal Tashchit* injunction, prohibiting a besieging army from destroying the fruit trees of the besieged. The rabbis also had a strong sense of their environment, prohibiting, for example, the dropping of litter near human habitation. The continuity of the biblical and rabbinic message says to me that had the rabbis in their day been aware of impending environmental disaster they would have acted to engage all their community to strive to prevent it. If we remember that on these ten holy days we hope to be found worthy of confirmation in the book of life, we may then recall the phrase: *u-teshuvah u-tefillah u-tzedakah ma-a-virin et ro-a ha-gezeyrah* – but repentance, prayer and acts of justice may alter the weight of the decree.

In the context of today's climate emergency we may interpret this phrase as follows: the primary meaning of *teshuvah* is returning, turning back. We have become distanced from the natural world, we observe it on television or in our back gardens but we make little effort to do more. We need to return to a sense of kinship with the land, a sense that it is not a separate entity but an integral part of us. *Tefillah*, prayer, comes from a root meaning to judge oneself. We must scrutinize every aspect of our existence and become as environmentally responsible as we can. *Tzedakah*, meaning justice, and also balance, (before it gains the applied meaning of 'charity'), demands of us that we support those NGOs and charities trying to repair the damage that rapacious human generations have done to the world.

Do these things and we may alter the weight of the decree; we may bring our consumption, our destruction of creatures and habitat, our utilitarian sense of the planet, into a much more realistic place; then maybe, just maybe, our children and grandchildren will be able to live good, long lives in a redeemed world.

Kol Nidrei 5722
15th September 2021

Wisteria hysteria

Inheriting a garden from someone else can be a challenging business. Some of the shrubs and trees that the previous owners planted may not be to your taste and removing them can be a major undertaking.

Wisteria sinensis, as its Latin name suggests, hails from China; it arrived in London in 1816 courtesy of two members of the East India Company and within decades featured in many gardens. Some call it a tree, but it is actually a deciduous vine, and it can grow – brace yourselves, to 20-30 meters high.

To start with it looks harmless, and you train the spindly vines round whatever support structure you have put in place, and then you let it get on with doing what it does best, growing at a significant pace! The narrow green branches gradually turn brown, and then they grow, wider and wider; then almost before you know it they have spiralled round your support structure so tightly, with such a vice-like grip, that unravelling them is an impossibility.

Only two bits of advice if you contemplate having a wisteria – think long and hard about whether you can live with it when it is huge, and, don't plant it anywhere near household piping.

So it is beyond my comprehension as to why the planters of my wisteria, now a modest 30ft in height with a spread of 10 feet chose to plant it at the base of a major gas pipe, and a down pipe. It grows like a triffid, needs cutting back at least a dozen times each summer and is a constant source of anxiety.

Whenever I look at the twisted stems, entwined round the trellis next to which it was originally planted I am reminded of the habits we acquire as we age, especially those behaviour patterns that develop stealthily, of which we are almost totally unaware, and from which, by the time they have grafted themselves on to us with the grip of an anaconda, we would find it nigh on impossible to extricate ourselves.

One of the aspects of Sukkot that we often ignore is that of the window it offers us, some days after Yom Kippur has ended, to finally dispatch any sins for which we have not yet fully repented.

The 6th day of Sukkot is called *Hoshanah Rabbah*, which most progressive Jews ignore completely. Yet according to our tradition – and I see no reason why Progressive Jews should deny ourselves this opportunity – it is on *Hoshanah Rabbah* that the penitential season, which started on the first of *Elul*, **formally** ends. This is our last opportunity, in the context of the *Yamim Noraim*, to appeal for God's mercy and forgiveness.

This is epitomised by the physical act of removing the willow branches from the *lulav* and beating them on the ground or against a hard object until all the leaves have been dislodged. It isn't as easy as it sounds, it requires effort and exertion, and one or two of the leaves may still remain when we stop, out of breath and exhausted. The symbolism is powerful and perfect: even having gone through the Days of Awe we are still aware of the failings that grip us tightly, and which we may have refrained from admitting on *Rosh Hashanah* and *Yom Kippur*. So we beat the willow branches in a last gesture of repentance and when we cannot dislodge all the leaves we are graphically reminded that we will carry into the year to come some behaviours and attitudes that are to be profoundly regretted. Our task is to work on them as the months pass by.

So next Monday, if you are able, beat a willow or something similar until the leaves drop, and be reminded that your repentance from sin, albeit with some minor successes, will always be a work in progress.

Erev Shabbat Chol HaMoed Sukkot
24th September 2021

Remember, remember….

Remember, remember the 5th of November
The Gunpowder treason and plot,
I know of no reason
Why Gunpowder treason
should ever be forgot.

The nursery rhyme I learned when I was little, as did all of my contemporaries did not explain very much to me, though as I got older I came to understand that the 5th was really an opportunity for Protestant England to mount a symbolic pyromania pogrom against the Catholic Church. The Sussex town of Lewes, some 9 miles from where I grew up, took this to extremes, culminating in sending a burning tar barrel down the main street, symbolizing none other than the Pope.

Remembering is a powerful and resonant theme this week; last erev shabbat was Bonfire Night in the UK, this Tuesday the anniversary of Kristallnacht, yesterday Armistice Day and Sunday Remembrance Day.

The English verb to remember, is directly derived from a 14th century French verb *remembrer*, itself derived from a Latin verb *rememorari*. The Latin word has a meaning which explains what remembering is often about, to remember **again**. The act of remembering, or thinking again about something or someone, is often achieved by trigger mechanisms – objects, events, words, photographs – but there is no guarantee that what you remember will be what you might have expected to remember.

The solemn annual acts of remembrance in Whitehall on the Sunday closest to Remembrance Day, were historically presented as an opportunity to acknowledge the sacrifice of the casualties of World War One (and for some, to celebrate the 'glorious dead').

But the idea that remembering the millions needlessly sacrificed in the First World War would prevent another proved all too quickly to be false when the Second World War began a mere 21 years later. Arguably this was because those who negotiated the reaty of Versailles during the Spanish influenza pandemic did not remember the riggers that had started the original conflict and made many of the same errors as efore.

When the world discovered the horrors of the Shoah, the mantra was that by emembering what had happened future generations would be able to prevent such enocides occurring again. It was a brave hope, but ultimately a forlorn one. The bestial vil of Auschwitz-Birkenau and countless other Nazi death camps did not prevent enocide in Cambodia, Bosnia, Rwanda, nor will remembering them prevent further enocides in the future.

In some ways, the problem with remembering something is that it is a passive, nner process; and by definition something passive and internal is unlikely to see the ght of day. **We** practice a different kind of remembering because the Hebrew verb 'to member', *Zayin, Khaf, Resh,* has a plurality of meaning. Yes it means *'to remember'* ut it also means *'to mention, to name, to record, to consider'*.

True remembering cannot be an act of internal passivity, it must be active; it must ame what needs to be named no matter the embarrassment it might cause others; it eans to record accurately what needs to be recorded, it means to consider the utcomes of certain behaviours and their long term impact. Above all, remembering ust be about more than idle memories, it must demand action in the present.

November 5th, November 9th, November 11th, not just important dates to member, but symbols of human tragedy; and what about November 12th, today, the nal day of the UN's Cop26 in Glasgow? Will this date join the cluster of other ovember dates, and if so in what light? Will we remember it as the day on which a ansformative conference led to vital and binding international agreements that pegged lobal warming to a just about acceptable level? Will we remember it as the day stablished and wealthy nations agreed to painful measures in their own countries to rotect populations across the world facing an imminent existential disaster?

Or will we remember it as the day when a golden opportunity to preserve life on rth was wasted? A day when cynics condemned millions of precious, living beings death because they thought it was in their immediate political interest?

And if this is the case, will we use the extra meaning of the root *Zakhar* and name and shame those who will have cast a blight on our children and grandchildren, and on the planet on whose survival our own depends?

12th November 202

247 million

A news report on Tuesday caught my eye, the headline containing the eye-watering fact that a global survey had concluded that the population of sparrows had fallen by 247 million. There was some positive information about the growth of other avian populations, but none pacified me. Why? Quite simply because House Sparrows are my favourite birds. Growing up I loved the summer months when I could wake early in the morning and hear the sound of the Dawn Chorus; the predominant sound of which was the cheep and chatter of sparrows.

They are funny little things too, with their jerky movement, their belligerence and their call; and if you think sparrows are just boring little brown birds take a closer look. Their feathers are a combination of black and soft grey, russet brown and soft orange, their beak, bib and eyes jet black. They are tiny, only live for about three years, and are susceptible to the changes human beings have made in the urban environment where they once thrived. They also have an infectious manner that only the stoniest heart could resist.

In one of those moments of delightful synchronicity, the haftarah for *Parashat Vayishlach* comes from the book of Hosea, 11.7-12.12. In 11.11 there is the phrase: *ye-heerdu khe-tzippor mi-miztrayim*, translated by the JPS as *They shall flutter from Egypt like sparrows*. But the verb, *chet resh dalet*, has another, primary meaning. It means 'to tremble'. So, we may ask ourselves, why did the writer use this verb to describe sparrows? I have remarked before that the writers of the books of the Hebrew Bible lived in a world where there were far fewer humans and far more wildlife, and that they were acute observers of other species that appear accurately portrayed in their writings.

Now sparrows don't tremble in fear, but when they display, and when they beg for food, they certainly shake, and it seems obvious to me that an observer with a poetic turn of phrase could easily imagine them trembling.

Trembling, of course, can occur for many reasons: fear is a prime cause, but there are also involuntary shudders, trembling from stress and distress and anticipation.

Fear is a prevalent emotion in the Torah this week as Jacob prepares for hi inevitable reunion with his brother Esau; because he has a low opinion of himself h projects that on to Esau and is convinced that he is facing a huge threat to himself an everything that is his. The actual encounter is completely different from his expectatio however as Esau could hardly be more loving and generous-hearted. This is no surprising, so often that which we fear the most in anticipation turns out nowhere nea as bad as we had thought.

Nevertheless, the opposite reaction, over-weening self-confidence, denial of th facts that are in front of you, is at best foolhardy and at worst suicidal. And it has to b said that there are many, many things today that are legitimate causes for fear: th ebbing and flowing of Covid 19, the threats posed by a nuclear re-arming and genocida China, a reckless Russia, extremism of right and left and Islamist terrorism, risin nationalism, extreme weather events, global warming, economic destabilization acros the world that is a direct result of the pandemic, and that's just off the top of my hea

But if we can learn anything from Jacob's experience in this week's *sidra* it is tha fear can have a paralyzing effect on one's mind as well as one's body that makes takin the appropriate action almost impossible. Just because something makes us afrai doesn't mean it is going to beat us, it should charge all our senses, awaken all th resources we possess and goad us into effective action.

President Roosevelt famously remarked that '*we have nothing to fear but fea itself*', and even if that is not exactly apposite to our current circumstances, neither the slogan '*Be Afraid. Be very afraid.*' of David Cronenberg. We have to find a plac for ourselves somewhere in the middle of the two: realistic but not complacen energized but not paralysed, looking for solutions rather than giving up. In other word in this most 'interesting' of times, we need to hold our nerve.

19th November 202

All happy families...

Some of you may be currently watching the third series of the family saga called Succession. It is a drama featuring a family modelled – one suspects – on the family of Rupert Murdoch, the media tycoon.

The deeply unpleasant children of a deeply unpleasant man jockey for favour with their father as they try to cement themselves in place to take over his empire when he is finally no longer able to run it. We watched the first series, and it was compelling in horrible kind of way. But once it was over Gilly and I talked about it and agreed that watching people being vile to each other – even in a drama – was not really entertainment as we understood it and so we ignored series 2 as I am ignoring series 3.

The Guardian on Tuesday featured an article by a psychotherapist called Clay Cockrell who is a shrink to billionaires in the US. He describes the toxic excess on Succession as being true to the life of many of his clients: those who have made it to become rich beyond the wildest dreams of Croesus, and the children who have grown up without responsibility or achievement and no idea how to run a business or live a meaningful life.

He wrote: Succession is built on the idea of a group of wealthy children vying for who will take the mantle from their father – none of them are able to convince him that they can do it. And that is because they have reached adulthood completely unprepared to take on any responsibility. The wealthy parents I see, often because of their own guilt and shame, are not preparing their children for the challenges of managing their wealth. There is truth in the adage "shirt sleeves to shirt sleeves in three generations". On numerous occasions the child of a wealthy family has said to me: "We never talked about money. I don't know how much there is or what I'm supposed to do with it. I don't know how to take care of it. It's all so secret and dirty".

Now we would be hard-pressed to call the Patriarch Jacob a billionaire, but he was certainly a man of great wealth, gathered through his own deviousness and acuity.

His children, on the other hand, though they worked in the family business, were privileged, feckless and, on occasion, absolutely vicious. The family had been riven by feuds almost since the beginning: Jacob at odds with Laban, his father in law; Jacob's wives at odds with each other over who could provide their husband with more sons more regularly; Jacob's sons at odds with each other and all of them ranged against Jacob's favourite, Joseph. So deep was their enmity for him that when they got him on his own they came close to killing him.

This part of the saga of Abraham and his descendants, especially the portion *Vayeshev*, is rich in incidents and insights, and it is a potent reminder that of all the feuds, the hatreds, the loathing, none is worse than that between members of the same family. And once this type of interaction is normalized disintegration may not be that far away.

I have been watching, with mounting concern, the demonstrations across Europe against being vaccinated for Covid. Whatever the people are marching for, be they committed anti-vaxxers, civil libertarians, or anarchists, by rioting and attacking the police at their demonstrations they send out a signal to those who feel the same in all democratic countries. We are told by our governments that we may have to 'live with' Covid 19, as we live with 'flu, but most of us would rather be vaccinated to protect ourselves and others from a terrible illness. This means that those who oppose the rulings of their governments, particularly if they refuse vaccination, are a direct threat to us because of the risk of infection that they pose. That serves to weaken our society from within, to pit people against each other, and to destabilize our government and our country.

Joseph and his brothers were reunited, eventually, but only after years of pain, deceit and hurt. The divisions opening up in western societies may take a great deal longer to heal.

26th November 202

- 80 -

The most detailed discussion about the festival of *Chanukkah* in the *Talmud* can
e found, perhaps surprisingly, in the tractate called *Shabbat*. That surprise may be
iminished, however, by a moment's reflection on the fact that the two have candles
1 common.

It was never the finer detail of the rabbis' discussion that engaged me the most,
ither it was one phrase that, once read, has stayed in my mind ever after. The rabbis
ame to the conclusion that a *chanukkiyah* needed to be placed on a window sill so that
s lights could be seen from the street. Why? *Mishum parsumey nisa, so as to publicise
ie miracle*. What miracle? The fact that one little vial of oil was sufficient to last for
days.

Now the fact that the 'miracle' in question was something the rabbis deduced from
ie story in the book of Maccabees rather than from direct witness accounts is neither
ere nor there; a miracle was associated with the festival of *Chanukkah*, indeed it
ccupies a central place. So publicizing the miracle by putting the *chanukkiyah* on a
`indow sill did more than was intended, because it reminded every Jew who saw it,
:gardless of how wretched their lives might otherwise have been, that miracles had
een enacted by God in the past and could be in the present too.

People put things in their windows to send out a message these days too.

Whether it is something they believe to be funny, something about the security
/stem protecting their homes, support for a political party in a local or general
.ection, acknowledging gratitude to the NHS in the early months of the pandemic,
rotesting about something they don't like, or supporting a cause dear to their hearts,
iese notices **do** catch the eye of passersby and, even if only for a moment, are
:gistered by those who see them.

However, it needn't just be in our windows that we present or promote something,
iere are plenteous other means.

How we dress may inspire others to follow suit, (or move fast in the opposite
rection), what we say may have a similar effect; it is undeniable, however, that the

more prominent we are in society, be that local, national or international, the more responsibility we have to take for all the things we do.

Once, more, it seems, we are about to have our lives disrupted by the pandemic and its newest iteration, Omicron. We have been told by our governments that we 'have to live with' the Delta variant, accepting a certain level of risk in our lives that wasn't there before, and plenty of us have tried to do so. It has dented the confidence of many others who are now living lives very different from those they led pre-pandemic.

In these circumstances it is of vital importance that those in positions of influence set a good example to others about how to comport themselves in the face of such challenges and how to stay safe. It is equally true that those in positions of leadership who behave in a feckless and amoral manner can do great damage and, in the pandemic, even put the lives of others at risk.

In the UK, still wondering what the impact of Omicron will be on a national and individual level, we have an elected politician – I won't call him a leader – in the most important office of all, who refuses consistently and almost willfully to set the right example. He mouths the right words but never applies them to himself, he is a moral vacuum and as such cannot convince with a moral argument. Why does this matter to you? Because in a pandemic which may be with us for years, curtailing some of our traditional freedoms for the sake of staying alive, we all need a consistent, strong and unified lead. Without that, the forces of opposition, aided and abetted by anarchists, the far right, and the hackers of China and Russia, will steadily, inexorably, weaken our societies to the detriment of everyone.

It has been a relief for me, as I am sure for you, to leave the Covid subject to one side for a few months, but we are in a new situation now, and the stakes could not be higher, not just for our health but for everything else.

3rd December 2021

In the early 1960s a new zoologist began to capture international attention. She had gone to Tanzania at the invitation of Dr Louis Leakey, the world renowned paleontologist, to study chimpanzees at a place called Gombe. Her name was Jane Goodall. In partnership with her first husband, the film maker Hugo van Lawick, who worked for National Geographic magazine, she began a study which still continues; and even though all of her original chimps have died their descendants live on. The chimps of Gombe are the most studied wild chimpanzees anywhere in Africa, and the knowledge first garnered by Dr Goodall not only transformed the way in which the world saw chimpanzees but also gave us much food for thought about ourselves.

The key group of chimps was the F troop, under their matriarch Flo. There was also her deeply unpleasant son Frodo, a terrifying, murderous alpha male whose violent behaviour, so similar in some ways to that of human beings, she chronicled. She saw chimps wage war, use tools, and much more besides. The research done at Gombe has been transformative on so many levels, and the world owes Jane Goodall a massive debt. Now 87 years old, she continues to write and speak about chimpanzees, but in recent years she has acquired another persona as a result of the climate crisis and produced two hugely significant books – *Reasons for Hope: A Spiritual Journey* (2004) and *The Book of Hope: A Survival Guide for an Endangered Planet* (2021). Both are well worth reading.

In the Torah this week, Joseph's older brother Judah does something very brave; he stands up to the Egyptian vizier who is threatening to detain their brother Benjamin for a misdemeanor which Joseph has himself set up. He effectively puts his own life on the line for his brother, committing a deeply selfless act; his courage is so great that it smashes through Joseph's last reserves and makes him reveal himself, finally, to his brothers.

It is a seismic moment, everything hangs in the balance, it just needs someone brave enough to recognize that they are less important than the greater whole, and Judah steps up. It is a moment of hope.

As we contemplate a new iteration of the pandemic that has already changed all our lives, as we become more troubled by the global climate catastrophe that is already causing extreme weather events, so do we struggle to find hope in the future to overwhelm our fears for our children and grandchildren.

Listen to what Jane Goodall, another human being who made a courageous move when she was young which transformed not just her own life but that of millions of others, has to say about hope:

… if we get together and use our intellect and play our part, each one of us, we can find ways to slow down climate change and species extinction. Remember that as individuals we make a difference every day, and millions of our individual ethical choices in how we behave will move us to a more sustainable world…There is great hope for the future in the actions, the determination and energy of *young people* around the world. And we can all do our best to encourage and support them as they stand up against climate change and social and environmental injustice… remember that we have been gifted not only with a clever brain and well-developed capacity for love and compassion, but also with an indomitable spirit. We all have this fighting spirit – only some people don't realise it. We can try to nurture it, give it a chance to spread its wings and fly out into the world giving other people hope and courage….It's no good denying that there are problems. It is no shame if you think about the harm we've inflicted on the world. But if you concentrate on doing the things you can do, and doing them well, it will make all the difference (pp.232-3, The Book of Hope).

To which I will add a heartfelt Amen!

10th December 2021

lights of Fantasy

On this very day, a mere 108 years ago, something happened in Kitty Hawk, North 'arolina that was to change the world completely: two brothers called Orville and Vilbur, the Wright brothers, took the first flight in a fuel powered aircraft.

However exultant they were about their achievement, they could not possible have nagined what would happen in the years that followed or the astonishing evelopments within what became both the commercial and military airline industry. ircraft of all kinds have been made since those early days: mono-planes and bi-planes, pitfires and Messerschmitts, Caravelles and Jumbo jets, the Airbus 380, capable of king 853 passengers, and the Northrop Grumman B2 Spirit, commonly known as the tealth bomber, designed to be invisible to anti-aircraft defences. The progress in the st 108 years is extraordinary, and I wonder where things will go in the next century, naybe robot fighters being controlled by Artificial Intelligence, to name but one.

The phenomenon of flight is a cause of fascination to human beings; from a very arly age we become aware of birds flying through the sky and ask whether we could y like that. A simple 'no' rather than a complicated excursus on aerodynamics is the kely response: however, for those who remain fascinated by flight, the science behind and an explanation of it, it is something we pursue when we become older. Human eings have still not discovered a way to fly unaided, the closest thing to it that I have en is the wingsuits used by Base Jumpers, where a suit expands to resemble the skin aps of a flying squirrel, enabling the jumper to glide some distance before having to eploy a parachute and land safely.

The easiest, and safest, way to enjoy some of the sense of flying is through the se of drones. By a simple link between the drone itself and your smart phone you see 1 your screen what the drone sees as you direct its flight. When Hugo, my wonderful iddle grandson, demonstrated this to me one weekend in Wales I was entranced; were not convinced that any drone I flew would land up in a tree, or go through someone's indow, I would get one myself!

It often feels like looking down from a great height when we read some of the stories in the Torah.

I particularly have that feeling today, with the two major events in the final portion of Genesis, *Vayechi*. First, Jacob's blessing of his twelve sons, and then his death and ceremonial funeral procession from Egypt to the ancestral burial site at Machpelah near Hebron.

The first is full of drama; we see Jacob lying on his bed, surrounded by his sons all of whom are adults, some indeed quite elderly. They are there because they have to be, but the reluctance felt by some would have been borne out by the 'blessing' their father gave them – for one or two much more of a curse. I see them shuffling, looking at their feet, and also the difference between 11 dusty desert sheikhs and the magnificently dressed Egyptian panjandrum, Joseph.

The second is full of ceremony and dignity: Jacob's embalmed body is carried in state, with a cavalry and chariot honour guard, it is followed by Joseph and senior members of Pharaoh's court, then the brothers, their wives, children and grandchildren. It is a dramatic sight, vivid with colour, an appropriate ending for a long and diverse life, and for the seminal book in the Jewish literary tradition.

We cannot give ourselves the perspective of height to review what we do in our daily lives and how we do it. But it might be wise for us to keep in mind that a higher perspective could see things differently from how we see them at ground level. At times, if we can gift ourselves with these perspectives, we may well reappraise how we do what we do and become much more effective, and decent, as a result.

And of course, we should always remember that both these perspectives are what God sees, and if that doesn't act as the ultimate corrective I don't know what will.

17th December 202

Thought for the year

My dear mother, *z"l*, always used to dismiss the secular New Year: *it's just another day, a day like any other to all intents and purposes*, she would say. On many levels I agreed with her, but on one I could hardly disagree more.

As we know from Rosh Hashanah, we need moments in time when we stop to refresh and regroup, and even more important to assess and re-assess how the previous twelve months have unfolded. Our faith tradition tells us to do this every autumn, and secular society tells us to do it now.

So, what to make of 2021? For most of us this year will be, like 2020, defined by Covid-19. This year, notably, will be the year when restrictions were eased, for some of us way too much and way too soon; the much vaunted 'return to normality' was just a tabloid lie, a means for governments to escape from the crushing burden that dealing with the pandemic had imposed. Allowing people to live life 'like they used to' was always a huge gamble, and it was a gamble which we plainly and predictably lost.

In circumstances where Covid was still rife in the form of its Delta variant, especially in countries too poor to vaccinate their populations, it was always likely that a new mutation would appear, spread like wildfire in its country of origin and then begin to rampage through the global village.

So it is that Omicron, the highly contagious but potentially less serious new mutation, is backing Delta into a corner in the developed world, though this is far from the case elsewhere. The talk now is that Omicron, if it is the dominant variant, will infect the majority of the population, become endemic and then be like other coronavirus-based illnesses against which we get vaccinated once a year.

Over the last few months – my normal reading schedule has been trashed this year – I have been reading a fascinating book called *Aftershocks: Pandemic Politics and the End of the Old International Order*. Written by two American strategic policy experts, Colin Kahl and Thomas Wright, it compares the Covid-19 pandemic with the Spanish flu pandemic of the early 20th century.

It is a well written and engaging read, and some of the parallels between the two, not so much in terms of illness but of impact, are sobering, and convincing.

One of the most important impacts, both of Covid and Spanish flu, is on global trade, not just in terms of the havoc wrought in business but also in terms of human misery as businesses pulled in their horns dramatically and millions of people lost their jobs. If you think that every job lost adversely affects several human beings rather than just the job holder you begin to appreciate the enormous social, as well as economic impact of the virus.

One of the effects of Spanish flu was that it broke international trade apart, countries and economies became less interested in trading with the world and became inward looking and protectionist: and protectionism inevitably leads to nationalism, and we all know where nationalism leads.

A few days ago, in its current spat with the EU commission, a leading Polish politician stated that the EU was becoming "a fourth Reich under German hegemony". This language is incredibly inflammatory, and calculatingly so, and it must not be dismissed as a national politician sounding off; it is a call to the nationalist spirit of the Polish people and represents a huge threat, not just to the relationship between the European Union and its members, but also to the stability of Europe.

If we end this ghastly year with any overriding thought, it should be an acknowledgement that pandemics do much more than kill their human victims, they threaten the nature of national and international politics, they encourage nationalism and are a threat to world peace.

We must be aware, call out protectionism or nationalism when we hear or see it and never forget that in isolation there is no life.

I wish you a safe and healthy 2022.

31st December 2021

ello Darkness, my old friend…

Try looking for popular songs which reference darkness and you will be spoiled
or choice, though the only one I could think of unaided was Simon and Garfunkel's
pening line of The Sound of Silence, *Hello darkness my old friend*. On the other hand
here are plenty of words for darkness of different kinds in biblical Hebrew: there are
9 occurrences of words meaning dark in the Tanakh and 151 meaning darkness.

Most of us will recognize *Choshekh*, which has two derivatives *chashokh* and
hasheykhah; but what about *emesh*, an old word also found in Akkadian and meaning
esterday evening, *alatah* meaning to be covered in darkness, *yamesh choshekh*
eaning darkness so thick you could touch it, and *tzalmavet*, wrongly translated by the
ing James Bible as 'valley of the shadow of death' but actually meaning thick
arkness and with another Akkadian cognate, *tzalamut*, meaning the same thing.

Why all this stuff about darkness? Mostly because the plague of darkness, the
enultimate assault by God on Pharaoh, is detailed in this week's Torah reading, but
so because in the UK this *Shabbat* has been designated Mental Health Awareness
habbat. Now it would be possible to have every *Shabbat* of the year designated for
mething or other, so popular have these designated days become, and I rather resent
lot of them for their *chutzpah*.

That does not at all apply to Mental Health Awareness *Shabbat* which is an
portant opportunity to raise understanding of something that affects us all in one
ay or another. Indeed it is regularly reported that some 20% of the UK and Irish
pulation suffer from depression, although there are other more serious mental
nesses such as manic depression, bipolar and schizophrenia.

There is a much greater understanding these days of mental illness compared to
ars past; back then a standard response from a doctor to a depressed patient would
ely have been 'pull yourself together man!', and those with other ailments would as
ely have been sent to an asylum because they would have been deemed unfit to live
mainstream society. Thank God those attitudes are unacceptable today, and that

modern medications can enable many with a mental health issue to function well in th world.

Nevertheless there is still a stigma attached to depression in some circles, eve though many well-known people have, through 'outing' themselves as suffering fror depression, lifted understanding of this as a mental illness rather than a 'bad day'.

Darkness is a very good metaphor for depression, thick darkness you feel you ca touch even more so, because those who are depressed can feel enveloped by an inne darkness that is incapacitating and which, without chemical help, can be hard to shif Nothing can cheer you up, nothing can make you 'snap out of it', things you enjo doing at other times leave you cold, you are mired in darkness and cannot move.

Many people suffer from depression, everyone knows someone with a ment health issue of one kind or another, and raising awareness gives them an opportunit to broaden their minds as well as their understanding. Two named biblical figure suffered from depression – King Saul and the prophet Jeremiah; Jeremiah writes of th agonies he suffers, even going so far as to say that he wished he'd never been born. would defy anyone to read that and not be moved to the depths of their being.

There is room for hope however: a wonderful young doctor in Harrow, Davi Lloyd, told me one day in 1999 that I was suffering from severe clinical depression b gave me the good news that it was treatable. He spoke the truth even though, some 2 years' later I am still on a very high dose of medication and will be for the rest of m days. Nevertheless it enables me to live, to work, to find joy and hope, and to avoid th thick darkness which had a habit of enveloping me over many, many years.

So this Mental Health Awareness Shabbat all I can ask of us is that we open ou hearts and our minds, to show understanding and compassion for those who, in th Torah's words 'grope around in thick darkness when it is noon'. (Deut.28.29)

7th January 202

Acknowledging the inspiration of student rabbi Daisy Bogod for this Thought F The Week

Seeing the Woods and the Trees

In the Sussex countryside that will always be my spiritual home there is a landmark spot that I visited many times with my parents. It is called Chanctonbury Ring and is an iron age fort on a 242m high hill on the South Downs Way. Throughout my childhood and adolescence it was also notable for the circle of massive beech trees which formed a crown around its summit. They had been planted by a landowner in the mid 19th century to beautify the spot further – very successfully – and when I first encountered them as a toddler they were just over 100 years old.

Standing beside a beech tree when you are small is a wonderful experience. Its smooth bark draws your eyes upwards to the canopy of leaves which let beams of sunlight through as the breeze blows. It also reminds you of how small you are in comparison with such a natural wonder.

In 2006, for my fiftieth birthday, Gilly and I went to the Sequoia and Kings Canyon National Park in California. Seeing the giant redwoods had been a childhood ambition but when I saw them for real rather than on film or in a stills photograph, the emotion I felt was one of sheer awe, a powerful physical and spiritual feeling.

It is not just the sheer size of some of the trees: the General Grant, for example, is close to 2,000 years old, just over 268 feet high, and with a trunk circumference at its base of just over 107 feet. The biggest tree in the world is also in the same forest, named the General Sherman, it is just over 274 feet high and has a base circumference of just over 102 feet. And it is dated anywhere between 2000 and 3000 years old. That means it was a sapling at the start of the Bronze age, when the great pyramid of Khufu was being constructed, Stonehenge was newly built, and the Kilternan dolmen was under construction.

And if that thought isn't enough to blow your mind, think about everything that has happened in human history during the lifetime of the Sherman sequoia and then lie down for a bit somewhere quiet.

One of the things you cannot but notice when walking around the giant sequoia forest is the amount of fire damage.

Most of the great trees have been burned in wild fires, but their huge size has enabled them to carry on, like someone with a terrible wound that has nevertheless healed. But just as we carry scars from such injuries so do the burning scars on the sequoias, as a sign of both their fragility and indomitableness.

The Generals have not always been the largest trees in the world, others that were even bigger have been measured but they have been destroyed, usually by fire, making the Generals' survival all the more impressive.

The beautiful beeches of my Sussex childhood were hit by the hurricane that cut a swathe through southern England in 1987. Thousands and thousands of beech trees were felled, uprooted as if by a willful giant, lying across the ground where they landed reminiscent of dead bodies after a terrible medieval battle. Only a dozen beeches on top of Chanctonbury Ring survived, looking like a quiff left on a man's head after the rest of it has been shaved.

The first visit I made to Hove after this carnage occurred was almost a physical torture as I drove down the A23 and saw those glorious trees reduced and destroyed. The terrible California wildfires of 2020 and 2021 wreaked havoc with the forests in the north of the state, not least in its oldest park, Big Basin Redwoods, yet the great trees survived, grievously damaged in many cases but still alive.

It is Tu Bishvat on Monday, the new year for trees. Today we talk about massive reforesting projects to capture carbon dioxide as an essential weapon against climate change, so going and planting a tree is a *mitzvah* for both present and future.

But we should remember that trees, however large, are vulnerable, just as societies and their norms built over so many centuries are fragile.

We should never take for granted the survival of anything just because it has been around for a long time. All the things we take for granted, all that informs our society, all that is part of how we live, how we see ourselves, is vulnerable.

As the Psalmist said of human life, but which applies here too – *the wind passes over it, and it is gone, and its place knows it no more*. (Ps.103.15).

14th January 202

Live and Let Die….

There have been many editions of the Bible since the publication of the King James version in 1611. One of the most famous, not necessarily for the right reason, is that published in 1631 by the royal printers Robert Barker and Martin Lucas; known ever since as the 'wicked' or 'sinners' Bible there was a very unfortunate omission of a tiny word in the Ten Commandments. Unfortunately, when they came to commandment number 7 they omitted the word 'not' from *Thou shalt not commit adultery*. There must have been some very red faces the day the first complainant came to point out what they had done!!

It is however the 6th commandment that is prominent in my mind at the moment. It is also a commandment which has suffered from mistranslation: *Lo tirtzach* it states in Hebrew, to be translated in the King James Bible as *Thou shalt not kill*. That is not, however, what the Hebrew word actually means. The root is *resh, tzadi, chet, ratzach*.

The root itself has an Arabic cognate meaning to *crush* or *bruise*, but the Hebrew verb means to *commit murder*, and that is how the Jewish translations of the Masoretic text translate it. In this week in which we read the Ten Commandments from the book of Exodus, it is the 6th commandment which weighs on my mind.

Like many people in the UK, I have heard a lot about Ashling Murphy, the teacher and musician who was murdered while out jogging in County Offaly on the 12th of January. All murders are terrible, all are shocking, but this murder of a beautiful, 23 year old primary school teacher has, I know, shaken many in Ireland, as it has elsewhere. It has also redoubled calls for governments to crack down on male violence against women.

News of arrests in the middle of the week may well reveal more information but regardless of that outcome nothing can diminish the tragedy of such a senseless ending of a precious human life.

One of the toughest things that I have learned about death in recent weeks is its finality, a finality that the human mind takes time to comprehend.

How do you process the fact that someone who was not just part of your life but around whom your own life revolved has gone? Just gone?

It is very hard indeed in any circumstances, but when the death in question is of young person, their life barely begun, their promise huge, it is almost impossible t apprehend. And this makes coming to terms with such a loss a million times mor complicated.

I have always considered male violence against women to be one of the mos despicable acts a human being can commit; and many of those men who behav violently towards women do so out of hatred. There are far too many men these day who are angry with women, who blame women for the ways in which their lives hav turned out, rather than taking responsibility for their own failings; who consider wome and their role in society to be emasculating for them, who cannot cope in a compan which is an equal opportunities employer.

I can't help noticing something in that Hebrew root in the 6th commandmer meaning to *commit murder*. The Arabic cognate means to *bruise* or *crush*. Men wh seek to control women often lapse into violence: they bruise their bodies – and wors – as a way of crushing their spirits, and then too often they take the final, irrevocabl step of murder. Ashling Murphy joins the company of 244 other Irish women murdere since 1996, a staggering 87% of whom knew their attacker.

The Bible placed an injunction against murder between one to honour parents an another not to commit adultery. I would like to think that the ancients knew that th right way of leading a life that honours others is first learned from parents an continues in adult life. The law against adultery recognizes that deception in marriag is a devastating destroyer of trust; and it must surely be the case that the murder o another human being, especially when it is by the hand of someone known to th assailant, is the biggest betrayal of all.

21st January 202

"Details make perfection and perfection is not a detail" (Leonardo da Vinci)

Last weekend, the 43rd RSPB Big Garden Birdwatch took place. Gilly used to do this religiously so I am carrying on the tradition. The purpose of the Big Garden Birdwatch is effectively to take an inventory of our garden birds to get a sense of populations that are thriving or declining. Over the years the results have been fascinating and once they are aggregated form a very accurate picture of the state of our garden birds.

The idea is that you set aside an hour over the weekend to watch your garden and note how many of each type of bird visit you during those 60 minutes. The results may well reflect your location, and it is because all types of terrain and human habitation are covered that the RSPB can be confident of the findings. The public has until the 10th of this month to submit their results so we don't yet have the figures, but last year the RSPB reported that over the last half century some 38 million birds had been lost from UK skies. In 2021 the top ten birds were:

1. House sparrow
2. Blue tit
3. Starling
4. Blackbird
5. Woodpigeon
6. Robin
7. Great tit
8. Goldfinch
9. Magpie
10. Long-tailed tit

So what birds did I see? Blue tits, wood pigeons, starlings, house sparrows, a blackbird, a great tit, a collared dove and a wren. 6 out of 10 compared to last year's top ten. You may recall that I mentioned before my love for house sparrows which I discovered was shared by a number of others in DJPC; up until this year no sparrows had appeared in our garden, but this year, in time for the great garden birdwatch I had three for the first time and I hope they will be back! Now you can watch birds perfectly well with the naked eye, but the best way is with a pair of binoculars; with the right level of magnification you can see everything. Aspects of behaviour, how birds feed, the colours of their plumage and so on, give you a sense of the complete bird as the sum of all its parts. There are plenty of people who don't like too much detail, they find it boring, and they are not always wrong; but most of the time no one who studied anything closely will lose out from doing so.

Torah-wise, we are now at the stage of multiple details concerning the *Mishkan*, Israel's desert shrine. There is not a component part that goes unmentioned and from a design perspective it is a quite extraordinary structure. Yet I suspect for some, rabbi and lay person alike, there is just too much detail, it is almost suffocating, repetitious and boring. In a way, though, the detail is ultimately there to serve a higher purpose. We may concede that the likelihood of a group of nomads being able to build a structure of such complexity in the middle of the desert is pretty slim – the raw materials alone would have been hard to come by, so we need to ask what purpose these chapters in Exodus serve.

My answer is that the placing of the construction of the *Mishkan* in the time of Israel's desert wanderings was important because it was the source text for the Temple in Jerusalem, the prototype for something much more important. The Temple could not have been allowed to have even the faintest whiff of a vanity project, it had to be but the modern incarnation of an ancient structure, an ancient structure whose construction was commanded by God, and superintended by Moses and Aaron.

We all have a tendency to dismiss something that requires an effort from which we suspect we will derive little benefit, but I would argue that it is precisely things like this which offer the most. I was cold and numb after my hour doing the Great Garden Birdwatch, but I was elated by what I had seen, pleased to play a tiny part in a much bigger enterprise, and rewarded by observing the birds who had graced my garden, albeit briefly, with their presence.

4th February 2022

I recently finished reading a brilliant book called: *A (Very) Short History of Life n Earth: 4.6 billion years in 12 Chapters*. The author, Dr Henry Gee, has for the last ree decades been a writer and editor on the international scientific journal Nature. enry is an old friend who always had an engagingly quirky sense of humour, and his pproach in the book is to tell the story through key events and evolving organisms, so at the vast range of the years themselves does not overwhelm the reader.

As much as everyone loves to read about dinosaurs and the evolution of life on rth, it was other aspects of the story that interested me much more. Henry describes e enormous upheavals on the planet, not just before it hosted life forms but roughout the different 'ages'. Most intriguing was the story of Antarctica; at times ing covered in ice 2 km thick and at others having lush forests. But what really cited my imagination was the way Antarctica broke off from the super-continent ngea 30 million years ago and drifted steadily southwards until it came to rest over e South Pole.

Almost since the beginning it feels as if planet Earth has lurched from one extreme another: extremes of temperature, extremes of airborne toxicity, massive volcanic uptions like nothing that has happened during human history, and so on. And we are one such cycle right now, of which Henry Gee says: Homo sapiens had reaped the nefits, 2.5 million years into a series of ice ages that will last for tens of millions ore, and there will be almost a hundred such cycles before the ongoing series of ice es comes to a close. And he notes that of all the *hominins* that existed from 2 million ars ago, only we are left. Makes you think, doesn't it?!

Tomorrow morning the first event in a season of celebration marking the 120th niversary of Liberal Judaism will take place at the LJS in a shabbat morning service th a cast of thousands, live, recorded and on Zoom. The centenary happened on my tch at the Montagu Centre, the 120th under the aegis of the inestimable Rabbi arley Baginsky. In earth time a hundred and twenty years is nothing, but to us it eans a lot.

Now, any celebration of a major anniversary is inevitably an opportunity t
review the journey from past to present.

Twenty years ago as I recall there was a significant look to the past, remindin
ourselves of the principles of Liberal Judaism, of the founders, the early rabbis, and th
achievements of the synagogues that had mushroomed outwards from the LJS. I reca
much less being said about the future. Perhaps that is understandable, after all it is onl
the past that is knowable, the future is unknowable and unformed.

But looking back over the last twenty years it is safe to say that they wer
characterized by radical developments in many areas putting the voice of Liber
Jewish ethical monotheism front and centre in many of the most significant things th
have happened since 2002. Would the founders have understood all of these mor
actions – I believe they would have felt challenged by some, but once explained woul
have seen that the principles of these actions were merely a development of their muc
earlier radicalism.

As a Liberal Jew since childbirth, I am quite comfortable with radicalism, in man
ways I find myself ever more relaxed with it as I move towards old age. But there
still something else really vital that I feel very strongly about, and for some of th
impetus for which I owe my students at LBC, some of whom will be the Liberal rabb
of the future.

The founders of Liberal Judaism were deeply spiritual people, as their writing
readily attest, and I believe that there is a greater hunger for faith now than for mar
years. The pandemic has made all of us think much more about God, and the role Gc
may play in our lives, and whatever we do should be inspired by our commitment
ethical monotheism, which, by definition, combines faith in God with doing the rig
thing, at the right time, in the right way.

18th February 20

Exclusion Zones

The demilitarized zone between North and South Korea has become a wildlife haven. There are estimated to be some 6,000 different species in this strip of land which is 160 miles long and 2 ½ miles wide. Rare migrating birds flock there, and so do bigger animals such as deer and black bear. It is a potent reminder of what happens when human beings completely absent themselves from the land – wildlife floods back in.

A similar example, with even richer results, is the closed zone around the infamous former Soviet nuclear power station at Chernobyl which covers 2,600 square kilometres. Nature has taken over this vast strip of land because there are no humans in it, and on an even bigger scale. The Chernobyl exclusion zone has Brown bear, wild boar, wolves, Eurasian lynx, European bison, Przewalski's wild horses, elk and roe deer and a huge array of birds. Many of them may be contaminated by residual radioactivity but they have clearly found ways to take it in their stride and not produce hideous mutants.

The town of Chernobyl, of which most of us had never heard before the power station exploded in 1986, actually holds an important place in European Jewish history. Jews moved in to Chernobyl in the 16th century, and by the end of the 18th century it was a major centre for Chasidim, ruled by the rebbes of the Twersky dynasty. Many of them left there in the early 20th century because of pogroms against the community and by 1939 there were only 1783 Jews in the city. Chernobyl was occupied by the Germans between August 1941 and September 1943, and although many fled before the Nazis arrived all those who remained were murdered. The killings were done mainly by the infamous *Einzatzgruppen* and enthusiastically supported by Ukrainian nationalists.

The Twersky Hasidic dynasty had some eminent leaders: the first Rebbe, Menachem Nachum Twersky and his son, Mordecai, who was called the Maggid of Chernobyl, are two such, and there were others sufficient to put the small town of Chernobyl on the Jewish historical map in perpetuity.

During the Nazi occupation of Ukraine, many of its citizens collaborated with the Germans, serving as concentration camp guards, auxiliary police and in other capacities. But arguably the biggest stain on Ukraine's 20th century history is the fact that during the Nazi occupation some 250,000 Ukrainians enlisted to serve with the *Wehrmacht*, and a further 238,000 served in the SS. Ukrainian auxiliaries aided the *Einsatzgruppen* in rounding up Jews for slaughter, notably at Babi Yar, but in a number of other towns and cities as well. And the infamous Ukrainian People's Militia, among many other atrocities, murdered 7,000 Jews in Lviv, and nationalists were still rounding up and murdering remaining Jews in 1945.

In our time, and especially at the moment, Ukraine and the actions of Putin's Russia dominate every news bulletin and most conversations. We look with horror at the apparently inexorable descent into conflict and shudder at the potential loss of life. For many Jews, and particularly for students of Jewish history, there may be mixed feelings, and some may even see the coming cataclysm as payback for the crimes of the past. For others that may seem so far away as to be completely irrelevant.

Those who think that, however, are wrong. What takes place in Ukraine now and in the coming weeks and months will affect the entire world, and that is not something to contemplate in a detached way. One of the Chernobyl rebbes talked about the 'tiny ugly world'. The world has always been ugly, but it is now tinier than ever, everything is interconnected, and the current situation in central Europe should matter to us all.

25th February 202

On the 25th of October 1854, during the Crimean War between the British and the ussians, a battle took place at Balaclava. In the course of that battle 600 horsemen ere sent to prevent Russian soldiers from controlling over-run Turkish artillery. nfortunately due to the sort of cock up that often happens in war, the Light Brigade as sent towards the wrong guns, already manned by the Russians and extremely well aced. It was a slaughter house which cost the lives of 118 cavalrymen and 335 horses. ix weeks later, the Poet Laureate, Alfred, Lord Tennyson, published what has become ie of his most famous works, The Charge of the Light Brigade. It lauded the bravery f the brigade but clearly criticized the decision makers responsible for the catastrophe ith the phrase 'Not though the soldier knew someone had blundered'.

I was looking at a map of Crimea on Google Earth the other day and saw the name alaclava, and the poem then sprang to the forefront of my mind. It was a reminder to e that the British have history in that part of the world. The Crimean War, which sted for nearly three years in the 1850s, started over a simple religious dispute about cess to Catholic churches in Ottoman Palestine. By the time the conflict ended it had st as many as half a million lives.

But it is not just British imperial wars that have resonated as a result of the atuitous attack on Ukraine by the nasty little man in the Kremlin, it has been Jewish story. Kiev, Kharkov, Odessa, Lvov, Donetsk, Dnepopetrovsk, Uman and others sonate down the ages. And, of course, the Khmelnitzki massacres in the 17th century, hich cost tens of thousands of Jewish lives, happened in Ukraine.

We believe today that the world is more closely connected than ever before, and terms of technology that is absolutely correct; but the ties of Jewish history, the ties *Klal Yisrael,* connect us with Ukraine in a very particular way. That is not to suggest at it is an untroubled relationship, indeed it could hardly be so with the country that ntains Babyn Yar.

It can hardly be so when the second world war record of Ukraine shows it had a arter of a million citizens who served in the Wehrmacht and the Waffen SS. Yet we must also remember that 4 ½ million Ukrainians served in the Red Army and 250,00 served in Soviet partisan units.

Knowing this history is one thing, but it should not so squeeze our innate humanit that we are incapable of feeling pity for the sufferings of today's Ukrainians at Russia" hands, horror at the wanton destruction of Ukraine's cities and towns, and outrage a the deliberate targeting of civilians.

In one of those coincidences that cause a sharp intake of breath, this Shabbat i Shabbat Zakhor, on which we are enjoined to remember the dastardly deeds of th Amalekites towards the Israelites three millennia ago. The divine commandment in th book of Deuteronomy actually states: timcheh et zekher Amalek mitachat hashamayin you will blot out the name of Amalek from under the heavens. This injunction fal within Raphael Lemkin's definition of genocide as 'the deliberate killing of a larg number of people from a particular nation or ethnic group with the aim of destroyin that nation or group'. As a mitzvah it is on our statute book, something that many of ι find excruciatingly uncomfortable.

Genocide is a word that is used with far too little care these days, especiall applied to Mad Vlad, whose poisonous purpose is furthering his interests in the far ea of Ukraine. The Russian army is not big enough to control 44 million people, so it wi seek to achieve the little man's aims by pulverizing its infrastructure so that it become close to uninhabitable.

In the meantime, as the assault continues so will the outrage grow, so will th isolation of Russia continue, and even after the conflict ends, may it be speedily, it wi be many years before Russia is allowed to return to the family of civilized nations. Ar we must also acknowledge that our whole world has been changed at a dizzying spee and may never return to how it was. As Vlad's chum Xi in Beijing is likely to k thinking – may we live in much less interesting times.

Shabbat Zakhor 202
12th March 202

Virtual Reality

According to the Shorter Oxford English Dictionary, the word 'oxymoron' dates back to 1657. The OED defines it as 'a rhetorical figure by which contradictory terms are conjoined so as to give point to the statement or expression'. (Now often loosely = contradiction in terms).

There are legions of these, some funny, some serious, some so common that we don't even recognize them for what they are. *Intelligent government* is an oxymoron, s is *enlightened despotism, loosely packed, anxious patient* and *benign neglect. Peace ffensive* is an oxymoron, as is *original copy, relative stranger, religious tolerance,* nd *forgotten memories.* And of course, so is *civil war.*

Last weekend, however, I was introduced to a life changing oxymoron; for the rst time, thanks to friends, I encountered Virtual Reality.

Now I had a rough idea what Virtual Reality was: downloadable programmes that lay out on a screen before your eyes thanks to a head set. There are a great number of ese programmes already and more coming up all the time: you can play games in hich you are part of the action, visit different parts of the world, eaves' drop on onversations between people, watch marvelous documentaries and much more. But hat hooked me irrevocably was the short African wildlife documentaries for which othing could have prepared me.

A big screen opened up and then disappeared, and much to my initial shock I was anding in the African bush about four feet away from a leopard finishing a gazelle it ust have recently dispatched. It covered the remains and then moved off, pausing nly to give me a sideways look as it went. The scene dissolved and reformed, and as looked around I realized I was alarmingly close to an elephant which towered above e, and as I turned slowly on the spot I stepped back as another elephant, a massive ull, extended its trunk right at me, and then passed me by with what felt like inches to pare. The rumbling was something I could physically feel.

Finally, the scene reformed a third time and I was watching a female rhinoceros ith a little calf. I clocked quickly that Mum had a long and very pointy horn and she was looking right at me. She stood close by the calf which skittered about in a delightful way and then was joined by another full grown animal with which the first two went on their way.

At that point I decided that was enough and removed the headset, returning to Castleton in Wales. I spent the next hour semi-speechless and genuinely in awe of the experience I had had.

Something struck me particularly though: when my world dissolved and I was part of another I couldn't see my feet, and because that facility was removed I felt both unstable and vulnerable. Maybe that was because of the particular world I had entered after all the normal human response is **not** to stand a few feet from a bull African elephant? But I think we all need to feel our feet on *terra firma* to feel physically balanced and confident.

In these ghastly days, saturated with death and destruction in Ukraine, the real spectre of World War 3 and nuclear warfare and once more rising Covid figures, we may well question whether our Real Reality is actually more Virtual than we might think. It all seems to be so different from how life was a mere three years ago! Some of us participate like addicts in what is known as Doom Scrolling, moving from website to website, horror to horror, making us feel anxious, depressed and nihilistic; others avoid it all, or try to, but that is a hard position to achieve.

Virtual Reality is a wonderful means of escape from the ghastliness of the real world, to which we must inevitably return; but it is also a powerful reminder of the great truth that even with pandemics and a European war, we still live in a beautiful world with extraordinary people and places within it, with which one day soon, God willing, we hope to re-engage.

18th March 2022

Last Friday, an article written by the Jewish journalist Jonathan Freedland was ublished in The Guardian newspaper.

Against the backdrop of the indiscriminate bombing of Ukraine by Putin, he told family story:

It brings back a memory – or rather something fainter: an inherited memory, one at was passed to me.

Its origin is 27 March 1945; the 77th anniversary is a little over a week away. Early at morning, at 7.21 am, a V2 rocket landed on <u>Hughes Mansions,</u> a block of flats on allance Road in the East End. It killed 134 people, more or less instantly. Among em were two sisters, Rivvi and Feige (pronounced fay-ghee). Feige Hocherman was 3 and she left behind two children, a son not yet 11 and a daughter aged eight and a uarter. The little girl was my mother, Sara.

Freedland then went on to note that this was the last V2 rocket to fall on London, id, by the cruelest irony, of those 134 people killed 120 were Jews. And he added:

It meant that, as a very young child, I somehow thought "Vallance Road" :longed alongside Belsen or Auschwitz in the small lexicon of words to be spoken ily in whispers, each of them bywords for terror and grief. I was well into my 30s :fore I ever went close to that place. And yet, though I did not witness it and though only ever saw the physical destruction that bomb wreaked through grainy archive iotographs, I can honestly say that event shaped my life. Because it shaped my other's life. It made her who she was.

Freedland lovingly described how once grown up his mother went out of her way care for people, at the same time maintaining an implacable hatred of Germany and a equally unshakeable commitment to the state of Israel. Her empathy, her ability to ie above the deep scars of her childhood, and her indomitable spirit, all inspired her n and influenced his life.

So he knew, he said, how the impact of terrible events in one generation ca influence later generations with no direct experience of them.

As we continue to recoil in horror from events in Ukraine, at the flood of deepl patriotic Ukrainians fleeing for their lives to other countries, at the refugee familie deprived of husbands, sons and brothers, at the ever darker spectre of the use c thermobaric and hypersonic missiles, and the possible use of chemical or biologica weapons, we can only wonder how awful this has to get before a ceasefire is called an real peace negotiations begin.

And we would be unwise to think that the free world may not feel, if chemica weapons are used illegally in Europe by Russia, that it has to stop the Russiar whatever it takes. God forbid, because it might be the end of most of us, but shakin our heads while doing nothing is not going to be enough for very much longer.

Parashat Shemini in the book of Leviticus is the *locus classicus* for the ke aspects of the dietary laws. We are told what we can eat and what we cannot eat, bu we are not really told why this is the case. The hardest commandments to fulfil, we a told, are those which have no rational explanation, you just have to do them becaus the Torah says it is God's will.

Wars kill people, not just soldiers but non-combatants also. There is no bigg taboo in peacetime than taking the life of a human being; but the faiths do allow f killing in wars of national defence, what Christianity labels 'just wars'.

What is happening in Ukraine is not a just war. Russia is not defending its nation life, it is prosecuting a war started by a nasty little despot to suit his personal purpos and because he is utterly without moral scruples, he has no qualms about the weapor he uses or on whom they fall.

The free world's response to date has broadly been magnificent, but ultimate may not prove enough. The scars of this time will be etched on our psyches, an *inevitably*, on our children's and grandchildren's also.

25th March 202

The Writing on the Wall

The first piece of graffiti in recorded history has an illustrious pedigree, in that the writer was none other than God! The writing in question was *Mene Mene Tekel Ufarsin*, often translated as 'You have been weighed in the balance and found wanting'. The wall on which the writing appeared, according to the book of Daniel, was in the palace of the Babylonian King Belshazzar, and announced the fact that he was about to lose his empire.

There is barely a civilization or an age which does not have its graffiti, and if anyone thinks that it is a modern phenomenon they could not be more mistaken.

In more modern times graffiti has definitely had a subversive element to it, particularly when it appeared on the walls of buildings in a country ruled by a dictator; and even in democratic countries there were no doubt those who huffed irritably when writing appeared on the wall. But over the last two-three decades attitudes have changed and graffiti is considered by many to be an art form.

Anyone who has seen some of the graffiti in Dublin, or Berlin or New York will know that some of the images, even when they are just letters are at least eye catching. And there are others who have taken the graffito and transformed it into a work of art worth hundreds of thousands, and occasionally millions, of pounds at auction.

Most of us have heard of the elusive Banksy, whose actual identity remains unknown but whose work over the last few years has delighted, challenged, shamed and embarrassed, as appropriate to its viewers. He has also had a knack for popping up in unlikely places and leaving behind something very powerful, as he did at Marble Arch in 2019, during the Extinction Rebellion demonstrations in London. Fewer know of the Puerto Rican Lee Quinones, the Italian BLU, the American Lady Pink, or the Brazilian Oz Gemeos, but they are widely considered to be among the greatest living graffiti artists.

The other day I had to drive through the Cambridgeshire town St Neot's, which is about 20 minutes from where I live.

There is an old fashioned barber whose back wall abuts a car park, and I have to drive past it to get to where I usually go. In the last two years they have had an arrangement with a graffiti artist called Jonny Graffiti. The last one I remember was of an underwater scene at a tropical reef, with fish in a multiplicity of colours, created in such a way as to appear three dimensional. It was breath-taking, like looking into giant fish tank, and I was most impressed.

But the new one capped them all. Set against a sky full of clouds tinged pink by the sun, there was a giant dove, holding in its beak not an olive branch but a twisted piece of cloth, coloured yellow and blue, the colour of the Ukrainian flag. Beautifully executed, a simple image drawing the eye instantly, and a message both powerful and poignant.

It is astonishing to see the way in which the conflict in Ukraine, and particularly the suffering of the Ukrainian people, has captured the hearts of millions. The picture of the dove, in a strange way, expressed this powerfully; I say strangely because what made it was the twist of colour in the bird's beak. It could have represented the Ukrainian flag, plain and simple, but the fragment, so twisted, spoke for me of the terrible damage inflicted on the nation defined by that flag; but the way the bird was soaring into the high heavens combined to say that battered Ukraine was not yet broken and would rise again.

With graffiti art, as with life in general, it is often the small details that convey the most, providing you pay attention!

1st April 2022

here but for the grace of God…

In the *Haggadah* immediately preceding the one currently in use within Liberal Judaism, there is a powerful short meditation by John Rayner Ztz"l, which reads as follows:

We were strangers in Egypt and Kiev, we were foreigners in Babylon and Berlin.
We were outsiders and wanderers in Spain and Poland and France.
We looked at the citizens of those lands with the dark, pleading eyes of the alien.
Our hearts beat the hesitant beat of people without rights, fearful and uncertain.
We pray that You help us to remember the heart of the stranger when we walk in freedom.
Help us to be fair and upright in all our dealings with everyone.
Oh burn and brand the lesson of all the years and all the lands on our hearts.
Eternal God, make us forever strangers to discrimination and injustice.

I have always loved this piece, and read it at every Seder using the ULPS *Haggadah*. It spoke to me of the dark times in Jewish history, and of the responsibility of those privileged to be born free and live in a free society to empathise with the poor and marginalized, the refugee from oppression or terror, and those whose lives have been turned upside down and emptied without any blame resting upon them for their fate.

I never expected that in 2022 we would be preparing to celebrate the festival of *Pesach* with more refugees on the move in Europe than at any time since the Second World War. The response to the refugee crisis engendered by the war in Ukraine has been extraordinary; ordinary families in many nations have agreed to sponsor refugees, individuals and families, indeed citizens have often been much more open, and generous, than their governments. Nearly four million Ukrainians have fled their country; the UK has offered 25,500 visas, and the Irish Times noted a few days ago that 17,000 refugees have come to the country. I have to say that on the basis of thi the verdict on the UK has to be – must do better.

Mind you, as Jewish families in the UK discovered when they took in Germa Jewish refugees before the Second World War, having a foreigner in your home, eve if you have some things in common, is not easy.

One of my colleagues in Belgium recently sent out this heartfelt plea:

> I'm looking for some simple resources in Ukrainian or in Russian to explai the basics of my job to my non Jewish Ukrainian guest who does not speak a wor of French or English. My main point would be the idea of Shabbat (not rules) an Pesach including the prohibition of having Chametz at home. I guess it's going be tricky to explain why bread, rice, pasta and beer will not be welcome in m home for a week!

We often say that Passover is the foundational festival of Judaism, and that i message about the refugee and foreigner is timeless. This year, if we ever needed i offers the proof of that truth. We are commanded, not requested, **commanded** to ca for the refugee and the stranger 'because you were refugees in the land of Egypt'.

This year we really have a reason to live up to our past as a people and the messag it has for us. Find out what you can do to help those who have lost everything, gi what you can – money, clothes you no longer need, toys for the many children – a remember that with every Ukrainian refugee, adult or child, that you help you will l fulfilling one of the most important teachings that Judaism has – to remember that yc were refugees in the land of Egypt.

8th April 202

The Zebra's Hoof

Some of you may remember me telling you about an extraordinary zebra foal, born in the Serengeti a few years ago. It was unlike anything that I could ever have imagined. Instead of the deep brown stripes on a white background that we would associate with a standard Zebra of any of the breed's 3 sub-species, the foal was brown with white spots. There are colour mutations in animals – the albino being the most widely known – and arguably the most magnificent of which is melanism in big cats, leading to black leopards and jaguars, and very, very rarely tigers.

Colour mutations in zebras, paler coloured stripes and mane, are not as unusual as might be thought, but a spotted zebra is still a breathtaking sight, and as likely as not also a high visibility target for predators. Yet the last reports I could find of the spotted 'foal no longer' did not report its consumption by lions, leopards, hyenas or African wild dogs.

By a happy chance, I went a couple of weeks ago with my wonderful grandson Hugo, to a small zoo in Norfolk that had successfully bred two Siberian tiger cubs last November. We had a good walk round, and I took several hundred photos; when I got round to looking at the pictures I was particularly pleased with the ones I had taken of a handsome pair of Plains Zebra. As I scrutinised them I suddenly noticed something had never seen before.

If you look carefully at a Zebra's hoof– not something, I readily accept, that any of us get to do on a daily basis – you will see that just above the hoof itself, at the base of the hock, there is a cuff of fur that is brown and has white spots. So it begs the question as to whether a Zebra is a white animal with brown stripes or a brown animal with white stripes?

It got me thinking about the importance of detail and context, how important they are in the grand scheme of things and how easily we forget about them; and in forgetting them we fail altogether to see what may be right in front of us, or we misconstrue it completely.

Synagogues, be they in brick or online, are not monoliths, they are not objects or formless entities; synagogues, as **we** have discovered over the last two years, can be as effective in the virtual world as they are in the real world, in a way we could never have imagined: why? Because a synagogue is made out of people, and there are many ways in which people can join each other and feel bolstered, cherished, even enriched by so doing. Sometimes we can't see the people for the building; sometimes we voice our frustrations at 'the synagogue' and forget that the target they hit is not an inanimate wall but living, breathing human beings with feelings and sensitivities. Now, we have no excuse to do so.

Reflecting back on the last two years particularly, what we may one day call the 'Pandemic' or 'Online Years', I take with me some experiences born of adversity and necessity that are intensely precious. I have been allowed in to your homes, have led services aware of the movement that goes on when anyone is on screen and closely observable. I have felt, in a way I can't fully explain, closer to everyone than I ever did a synagogue, and that has surprised me, especially as I would have always thought the reverse would apply.

When these Zoom services started I had my beloved Gilly sharing them with me, and I end them tonight on my own in a way, and in another way in your company and part of your company. It has strengthened me in the last two years and especially in the last 6 months, and I am more grateful for that than I could ever express.

As I think again about the spotty zebra foal, and the adult's hoof, I am reminded that the most important answers may be found in the tiny details, and that if God is anywhere it is there. I will never forget that discovery arising from DJPC online, and I hope that some of you will remember it too.

29th April 2022

The Final Zoom sermon, for now....

All the Right Notes

The composer Franz Liszt was born in Hungary in 1811 and died in Bayreuth in Germany in 1886. He was a pianist and composer of prodigious talent, not least much in evidence with his extraordinary transcription of all nine of Beethoven's symphonies for the solo piano.

Like other composers born into the Austro-Hungarian empire, Liszt was greatly influenced by Hungarian folk tunes, especially those of gypsy provenance, and his Hungarian rhapsodies are loved by many as some of the finest examples of the genre. I number myself among those many, and my particular favourite is his Hungarian Rhapsody No 2 in C-Sharp minor, the most famous of the 19 that Liszt composed.

My parents had a vinyl recording of the work, which Liszt also orchestrated for full orchestra, with the soloist Shura Cherkassky on piano. Cherkassky, born in Odessa in 1909, was an extraordinary pianist, a tiny little man who could make a concert grand piano do amazing things. He also recorded the Rhapsody for solo piano and it is one of my best loved pieces; the other day, however, I decided to do a compare and contrast exercise between Cherkassky and a couple of other fine pianists, Vladimir Horowitz and Alfred Brendel.

Cherkassky plays to all the subtleties of the piece, gentle in some places, powerful in others; Horowitz, playing the piece as an encore after one of his recitals, does not use the piano to explore the nuances of the composition as much as to blow it up. He is heavy-handed and unsubtle, his tempi and phrasing being, as was the case with so much of his performance, all about pianistic shock and awe, all about him rather than the piece itself. Alfred Brendel, as his devotees – myself included – would expect, performs the piece as an act of homage to its composer, bringing out tiny aspects that the others ignore, and creating a memorable rendition. I have no way of knowing whose performance would have pleased Liszt the most – I fear Horowitz's – but that doesn't mean very much as, like so much else, this is a subjective matter.

Listening to the same piece of music performed by different artists can be an engrossing exercise, and a potent reminder of how the same thing – in this case musical composition – can be rendered differently, and in that difference joy may be found.

For most of us it is not pieces of music as much as life itself which we approach in our individual ways. In our childhood we are influenced most by our parents who, having learned the hard way about life and how to live it, seek to guide us to do the same thing. By and large that works until we hit adolescence when we discover that there is more than one way to approach life, and the way we have been taught by our parents will be an incentive to try a completely different one! And from our success or failure much will be learned.

The greatest truth, of course, is that there are as many ways of approaching life as there are human beings, and religious life – which acts like parents to regiment our behaviour – will chime or not with each person depending on their makeup and life experience.

Like life, our engagement with an ancestral religion starts when we are born and stays with us through the rest of our lives if we are so minded. It has its shared points along the path of life, baby namings, *Bnei Mitzvah*, marriage and death, and each year punctuated by sabbaths and holy days which reconnect us to ancient traditions and make us part of the great chain of religious transmission that binds the generations.

And in our individuality, within a religious structure, we make ancient traditions personal, we add ourselves to them and make them even more special and meaningful; this weekend we witness Asher at the start of his journey, and Anna marking an important milestone on her path to adulthood.

In life, as in playing the piano, you may or may not choose to play the right notes in the right order, but that you will still make music is beyond dispute, the music of your life, the music of your soul.

27th May 2022

Baby naming of Asher E and before the Bat Mitzvah of Anna R

Glossary

Pesach: Hebrew name for Passover

Sedarim: Hebrew, plural of Seder, the name of the ceremonial meal on the first evening of the Passover festival

Toi, toi, toi: a Yiddish term to ward off the evil eye

Keyn yehi ratzon: Hebrew, may this be His (God's) will

Tazria-Metzora: name of the double portion, 4th and 5th, of the book of Leviticus Chapter 12.1- 15.33

Captain Sir Tom Moore: 1920-2021. Centenarian D Day veteran who raised over £32 million pounds for the NHS during the Covid pandemic

Albert Camus: Algerian born French philosopher, 1913-1960

Gabriel Garcia Marquez: Columbian novelist, 1927-2014

Tanakh: Hebrew acronym for Torah, Neviim, Ketuvim – the Hebrew Bible

Prozbul: derived from a Greek word, the *prozbul* is the name given to a mechanism created by Hillel the Elder, 1st century BCE; a legal device to avoid the cancellation of debts in a *Shemittah* (sabbatical) year

Kehillah Kedoshah: Hebrew, holy community, generic name for a synagogue

Mishneh Torah: Maimonides' great codification of Rabbinic *halakhah*

Moses Maimonides: 1138-1204

Pikkuach nefesh: Hebrew, Saving of Life; the suspension of the strictures of Shabbat observance when there is a threat to life or health

Yamim Noraim: Hebrew, Days of Awe, the usual Hebrew term for the High Holy Days of Rosh Hashanah and Yom Kippur

Simchah: Hebrew, joy, celebration

Sifrey Torah: Hebrew, Torah scrolls (lit. books)

Der Stürmer: Nazi propaganda paper edited by Julius Streicher, 1923-1945

Mensch: Yiddish from the German word for a man, in Yiddish applied to an exceptional human being of either gender

Shehecheyanu: Hebrew, a blessing for special occasions

Mar: Hebrew, bitter

Marcheshvan: 8th month of the Hebrew lunar calendar

Vayeyra: fourth portion of the Torah, Genesis 18.1-22.24

unserer: German/Yiddish, our own

JPS: Jewish Publication Society (of America)

Zohar: the great text of Jewish mysticism

Lulav: Hebrew, palm, but also the inclusive name for the four species – palm, myrtle, willow and etrog (citrus fruit) that are ceremonially waved at the festival of Sukkot

Bal Tashchit: you shall not destroy, concerning the wanton destruction of fruit trees during a time of conflict. Deut.20.19

President Roosevelt: Franklin Delano Roosevelt, 32nd President of the USA, 1933-1945

David Cronenberg: Canadian film director, born 1943

Khufu: second Pharaoh of the Fourth Dynasty, builder of the great pyramid at Giza, 2575-2566 BCE

Stonehenge: Neolithic stone monument on Salisbury Plain, constructed between 3000 and 2000 BCE

Kilternan Dolmen: a megalith in County Dublin, believed constructed around 2500 BCE

Klal Yisrael: Hebrew, literally, All of Israel, but in an applied sense, the Jewish people

Vlad Vlad: President Vladimir Putin, President of Russia 2000-2008, 2012 –

Shabbat Zakhor: the Shabbat before the minor festival of Purim when Deut. 25.17-9 is read in addition to the regular Torah reading.

Raphael Lemkin: 1900-1959. Polish born lawyer who coined the word genocide.

Xi: Xi Jinping, Chinese President since 2013

Haggadah: Hebrew, the liturgy used at the Passover Seder

John Rayner: Rabbi John D Rayner, CBE, born in Berlin in 1924, died in London in 2005

Tz"l: abbreviation for Hebrew *zekher tzaddik livrachah*, the memory of a righteous man is a blessing

Seder: see Sedarim above

ULPS: the Union of Liberal and Progressive Synagogues, UK based Progressive movement now called Liberal Judaism

Shura Cherkassky: 1909-1995

Vladimir Horowitz: 1903-1989

Alfred Brendel: b. 1931

Afterword

These thoughts, shared with my community in Dublin, were delivered from the start of lockdown in March 2019 to April 2022.

During that time I was largely at home, working and also caring for my wife Gilly, who had a serious illness and died in late October 2021.

She heard many of these texts at the same time as my congregants, and always gave me helpful suggestions and feedback. Her death has opened a hole in my soul that can never be filled, but I shall always be grateful that circumstances conspired to give us nearly two years of 24/7 time together at the end of her life.

We were friends and soul mates for 40 years, and my love for her will only end when I do.

Charles Middleburgh
Leo Baeck College
September 2022

Printed by Printforce, United Kingdom